FIFTY

D · A · Y

SPIRITUAL

ADVENTURE

FIFTY
D · A · Y
SPIRITUAL
ADVENTURE

Successful Steps for Transforming Your Daily Work

by the "Chapel of the Air" team:
David & Karen Mains
and
Steve & Valerie Bell

MULTNOMAH
Portland, Oregon

Cover design by Bruce DeRoos & Paul Clark
Edited by Steve Halliday

FIFTY-DAY SPIRITUAL ADVENTURE
© 1989 by David and Karen Mains
Published by Multnomah Press
Portland, Oregon 97266

Multnomah Press is a ministry of Multnomah School of the Bible, 8435 N.E. Glisan Street, Portland, Oregon 97220

Printed in the United States of America

Library of Congress Cataloging-in-Publication Data

Fifty-day spiritual adventure / by David Mains . . . [et al.].

    p. cm.
ISBN 0-88070-329-6
1. Vocation—Prayer-books and devotions—English. 2. Devotional calendars. I. Mains, David R. II. Title: 50-day spiritual adventure.
BV4740.F55   1990
242'.68—dc20   89-28584
                                           CIP

90 91 92 93 94 95 96 97 98 - 10 9 8 7 6 5 4 3 2 1

Contents

How to Use This Book

Habits—there are all kinds, both good and bad. Some people bite their fingernails. Others, as regular as clockwork, stop for a beer on their way home from work. Maybe you're one who habitually reads the Bible every morning or evening.

Habits. They certainly influence our lives! Because of bad habits people have been fired from jobs, lost at love, and failed to grow spiritually.

Conversely, because of good habits, others have disciplined themselves to learn difficult subjects, become master handlers of God's word, or have greatly improved their physical condition.

Habits significantly affect all our lives. Get used to eating the family dinner with the television on and it's hard to shut it off, even though experts agree it's a terrible habit! Make it a habit to live within your means and you avoid a lot of tension. Begin to regularly spend more than you make and soon you'll find yourself in desperate trouble.

It's because habits so significantly influence our lives that it's wise to establish good ones. Simple, right?

Let's do something about it! Let's embark on a fifty-day spiritual adventure that holds out the promise of remarkable growth, while also establishing long-range habit patterns.

But why fifty days? Why not twenty or thirty? We have found through our experience on the "Chapel of the Air" broadcast that fifty days is the optimum time to form habits that will remain with you once the adventure is over. You will not be the same person as when you began. Countless testimonies from participants in our radio adventures verify this.

The first spiritual adventure for listeners of the "Chapel" began back in 1980. That forty-day adventure, which attracted about seven thousand participants, has grown into an annual fifty-day adventure with yearly involvement of more than a quarter of a million people.

For each of us, these next seven weeks and a day hold the promise of renewed closeness to our Lord. We will discover an exciting reality: that Christ himself is with us in our daily work.

Practically everyone has some kind of daily work—business people, farmers, homemakers, students, the handicapped, retirees, even the unemployed and prisoners. How thrilling it is to realize that Christ is as comfortable in the workplace as he is in the church.

Now, adventures are not the same as vacations; adventures demand more concentration and more energy. There may be occasions when you will question why you began this quest. Undoubtedly there will be moments you'll be tempted to quit. Don't! Remember, adventures also involve exciting rewards and honor.

Most of all, a fifty-day spiritual adventure is a time for accelerated spiritual growth. Expect to sense a greater closeness to Christ by the end of these weeks. After all, that's what a *spiritual* adventure is all about.

This adventure is designed to begin on any Sunday. Each adventurer follows regular spiritual disciplines including prayer, Bible study, and showing Christ's love and kindness to those with whom he or she works.

The daily readings are the means by which we can have input into what's happening. Sometimes we based our comments on the Scriptures you're assigned; sometimes we didn't. We also invited three guests to help us out along the way.

While many people think spiritual growth means hours of intensive Bible study and forming calluses on your knees from long prayer sessions, that's not what this adventure entails. It requires no more than twenty to twenty-five minutes each day. That's not a lot of time! But the benefits you will reap from that small investment will seem amazing as the weeks progress. Once underway, you may be surprised at how easy the daily disciplines become.

One of the best things about this adventure is that you can measure your own spiritual growth. You will be able to track your personal progress.

Usually the first week is the hardest. If you keep up with the daily pace, chances are you'll finish strongly! But if you happen to miss a daily assignment, don't despair. Just get back on track with the next assignment. Remember—spiritual growth often brings on enemy resistance. On occasion you may find unexpected opposition.

If at all possible, try to get a friend to participate in the adventure with you. It's a lot easier to stick with it if you're not trying to go it alone.

Involvement in spiritual adventures is much of what following God is all about. Ask those who journeyed with the apostle Paul whether adventure marked his travels—you know the answer you'll get! And there's no question but that the twelve disciples had adventure fever when they left their fishing nets or tax tables to respond to Jesus' invitation. The things they left behind were mundane compared to working with the King in establishing his new kingdom.

The Old Testament is filled with this same adventurous spirit. Whether it's the daring exploits of David, the account of Israel's miraculous exodus from Egypt, or the narrative of Nehemiah's building project, all were adventures in the fullest sense of the term.

What marks all great spiritual adventures? *Enthusiasm.* Interestingly, enthusiasm in the Greek means "God-insideness"—the main elements of the word are *en* (in) and *theos* (God). When enthusiasm—"God-insideness"—marks what's taking place, the future will be characterized by excitement, fervor, zest, exuberance, expectation. What we need to push aside is apathy, aloofness, coolness, indifference, or a sense of detachment.

How's That Again?

Let's go over what's involved one more time—after all, this is not a normal book. It's not something you start reading and finish a day or two later. It's your guidebook for the fifty days of this spiritual adventure.

After reading about the five disciplines involved and understanding them thoroughly, you next need to decide what's going to be Day Number One for you. That's the date you will begin to read the Scriptures, pray the Ultimate Authority Prayer, do the End-of-the-Day Replay, etc. The Chapel team would suggest you make this coming Sunday Day Number One.

If the five disciplines are not clear in your mind, go back and reread them. If the adventure seems a bit intimidating, think about someone who might do it with you. Loneliness is no good. God saw that right at the start. Adam needed a partner, so God made Eve. Later we see Moses depending on his brother Aaron and his sister Miriam. David confided in Jonathan. Esther had her cousin Mordecai. Even Jesus found three special friends among his disciples: Peter, James, and John.

One of the more popular phrases in the New Testament epistles is "one another." Love *one another,* build up *one another,* bear *one another's* burdens. The Christian life is not lived only in the first person singular. It's plural. We need one another.

So find someone else to compare notes with, someone you can confide in, pray with, and support. As you meet together regularly, God will build both of you up. Remember that Christ said, "Where two or three are gathered in my name, there am I in the midst of them" (Matthew 18:20, KJV).

Where can you find such a person with whom to start a support relationship? Start by looking for a fellow Christian at work or in a similar profession. Perhaps someone in your church or small group Bible study would agree to do this. Young people might find such people in a campus or church youth group. You might even be able to carry on a support relationship by mail or over the phone. Once you've found someone, pray that God would help you build a mutually beneficial support relationship.

Finally, good adventures always include an element of the unknown. Many have reported to us a surprising resistance on the part of the enemy. They testify that they never before experienced such obvious spiritual warfare. Some of these same people have also verified a marvelous new awareness of the presence of Christ in their lives.

We covet this for you. Above all else, stay close to Jesus. We believe you'll experience the delight of seeing him starting to transform your daily work.

We are convinced that the Christian people of this land are at a crossroads. According to one Gallup survey, 42 percent of the people in this country are in church or synagogue every weekend, yet too few leave the sanctuary with a sense of excitement and adventure regarding the hours ahead. Our prayer is that this adventure will help us recapture a vision of how important we are as the people of Christ's kingdom.

This adventure is not make-believe. It's real. Christ is with us in our places of work. If there is holy enthusiasm throughout our ranks, what's ahead will be a glorious adventure indeed.

We fully expect the Lord to reveal himself through the various disciplines of this adventure. As we welcome him to our daily place of work, we're also expecting some miracles along the way. How about you?

KEY

D.M. – David Mains
K.M. – Karen Mains
S.B. – Steve Bell
V.B. – Valerie Bell

The Five
Disciplines

Bridge the Gap between Church and Work

It's a long way from Sunday to Monday. Sunday we dress to the hilt, study Scripture, talk and sing about Jesus, and enjoy warm Christian fellowship. But Monday it's back to the grind. If only we could bottle up some of that Sunday blessing and make it last through the week . . . if only our church life could invade our daily work life . . . if we could just bring those two worlds together!

Well, why not? Why does there have to be a Grand Canyon between Sunday and the rest of the week? Jesus is Lord of our whole lives. Our Sunday worship of him should spin off into six more days of active, nitty-gritty devotion.

Sunday is unique. We still meet Christ at church in a special way. But Scripture often warns us against Sunday-only religion. As we, the people of Christ's church, go out into the world, we must take our Savior with us.

The following are some creative ways to bridge this gap—ways to bring together the worlds of church and work. <u>Each week, choose to do one of them and record what you did in the space provided on that week's "Recording Progress" page.</u>

1. Bring something meaningful from Sunday-morning church to Monday-morning work—a verse of a hymn, a Scripture verse, a thought from the pastor's sermon, etc.

2. Tell someone at work one good thing about your church or pastor.

3. Start praying regularly for someone you encounter during your daily work.

4. Write out a brief description of a work-related problem you are facing and give this to your pastor so he can get a clearer picture of life outside the church.

5. Ask someone in your church about his or her daily work and visit that person's workplace if possible. The depth of your Christian fellowship will be enhanced as you learn more about what others in your church do each day.

6. Invite your pastor or a church leader to visit your workplace. He will know better how to minister to you as he learns more about your daily work.

7. Ask someone at church to pray for you regarding a work-related concern.

8. Apply a sermon idea to your work setting and let your pastor know what you did. Pastors need to know how their ideas translate into hands-on action in the workplace.

9. Share your faith. Tell someone you regularly see how Christ has changed your life. Or pass along a book, record, or tape that has enhanced your spiritual walk.

10. Write a short paragraph describing how Christ is transforming your daily work.

Discipline Two

Personalize Biblical Truths about Daily Work

Work is basic to human life; the Bible can't ignore it. We find Adam and Eve tending the Garden, Cain and Abel in their chosen professions, Noah pounding away on the ark, and Sarah fixing food for visitors. King David was a shepherd in his early years, and when Amos wasn't prophesying he was pruning fig trees. Later we see Jesus as a carpenter, surrounded by fishermen, homemakers, and tax collectors. Paul made a living by mending tents.

The most practical questions of the Christian life come up in our daily work. How hard should we work? How should we treat those around us? How should we act toward our superiors? What are our priorities? What about ethical questions on the job, stress, boredom, money? Scripture doesn't leave us floundering on these issues. As the Bible tells us how to live, it tells us how to work.

Each day during this fifty-day adventure, we will be studying a Bible passage that deals with work or some work-related issue. If your schedule allows, do this in the morning before your workday starts. In that way the biblical truths will undergird you throughout the day.

The important thing is to personalize the text of Scripture. It's great that God spoke to Nehemiah the construction foreman or to Martha the caterer. But what is he saying to *you* through each day's Scripture?

In the space provided for each day, write down what you sense God saying to you about your daily work. Apply the Scripture as specifically as possible.

Don't settle for "be nicer" when God is saying, "Don't get so ticked off at George when he makes too much noise." Take the time to listen for the Lord's specific instructions.

Reaffirm the Ultimate Authority of Christ

Who is your boss? Many of us have supervisors or foremen who oversee our work. For students, that role might be filled by professors or teachers. If you are retired or unemployed, you might be your own boss.

Many voices tell us what to do. It may be that the love of money is ordering you around. Or maybe it is pride. Possibly peer pressure is forcing your decisions. These are other "bosses" we encounter in our daily work.

Jesus wants to be our only boss, our highest authority. Throughout Scripture, the Lord repeatedly urges his people to turn away from other bosses and follow him. No one can serve two masters, Jesus said. We either follow Christ or antichrist.

Strong "two-boss" tensions are all around. For some, it is employers who expect their workers to be unethical. For others, the frantic climb up the ladder of success prevents their spending good time with their families. Whatever boss is giving orders, we need to reaffirm our allegiance to Christ above all others.

To help do this, <u>pray the Ultimate Authority Prayer each day. Make a copy of it and take it with you to work and pray it again as tempting situations arise.</u>

The Ultimate Authority Prayer

Lord Jesus,
You know I live in a "two-boss world."

Conflicting voices call for my allegiance,
but yours is the one I choose to obey.

Help me to please you today by
upholding your standards,
resisting temptation,
and faithfully representing you
in all I do.

I claim the promise of your presence this day
as I go about my work.
Christ, you are my ultimate authority.
Amen.

Reword the prayer if this would help you to feel more comfortable. Make this prayer your own as you think it through line by line. Try to understand it in terms of your own work situation. What standards do you need to uphold? What temptations do you face? How can you represent Christ more faithfully?

Discipline Four

Delight Others by Giving the Presents of Christ

Isn't it wonderful to get presents on your birthday? Just to know that someone cared enough to think about you, to buy a gift, to wrap it up, and to give it to you on your special day—that makes you feel good.

It's even better when the giver is Christ himself. He not only gives us presents, he *is* our present, because he gives his *presence*. Are you confused yet?

When Jesus lives in us, he fills our lives with his own characteristics—joy, gentleness, love, and much more. What marvelous presents these are! And they are even more marvelous when we give them away. We share Christ's *presence* with the people around us as we share Christ's *presents*. Got it?

Imagine how your work environment might change if you brought gift packages to give out. What would happen if the presents you gave were things like kindness and patience?

Three times a week, show one evidence of Christ's _presence_ in your life by giving one of these _presents_ to someone with whom you work. **Write down what you did for each week in the space provided on that week's "Recording Progress" page.**

Here are some of the presents we're suggesting:

1. *Faithfulness.* Think of this as loyalty. This might mean standing up for someone as others gossip about him or her.

2. *Gentleness.* A homemaker might make it a point one day to be especially tender with her children.

18

3. *Goodness.* Perhaps a salesman might decide to be particularly honest with his customers.

4. *Joy.* Do something crazy and fun to combat drudgery. Give away balloons or sing songs or write someone a nonsense poem.

5. *Kindness.* Do a good deed for someone who needs it. Be, like Christ, a servant.

6. *Love.* Your present of love may be a compliment, a prayer, even an act of giving yourself.

7. *Patience.* Make up your mind to bear with a co-worker even beyond what's reasonable.

8. *Peace.* Communicate this peace with reassuring words.

9. *Self-control.* Plan to keep from losing your temper at a bothersome colleague.

Discipline Five

Do an End-of-the-Day Replay

You expect "instant replays" of great plays when you watch a football game on TV. Through a miracle of modern technology, you can immediately see what went on moments earlier. With slow motion, you can even analyze the play step-by-step.

Replays not only benefit the fans, they also help the players. At some point the coach sits down with his players and reviews the game films. "Here's what you did right," he says, "and here's what you did wrong." As the players listen to the coach and apply what he says, they ensure their next performance will improve.

What if we lived our Christian lives like that? What if we could watch a videocassette replay of each workday? Imagine that. We plunk down in front of the TV with Jesus sitting beside us. His hand is on the remote control, and he's running the tape of the day's events. Occasionally he'll stop and review an event: "See, that person needed help and you didn't notice. Try to be more sensitive tomorrow." Or sometimes he praises us for a job well done: "You held your temper in that trying situation. Nice play!"

Does that sound farfetched? Well, the Bible speaks of Christ's Spirit doing just that sort of thing, standing beside us and reminding us of Jesus' instructions (John 14:26). It isn't outrageous to think that the Comforter or Counselor might also be called our Coach.

Here's your assignment: <u>At the end of each day, do a mental/spiritual replay in three basic steps:</u>

1. *Remove distractions.* If possible, get in a quiet place. Relax. Put out of your mind any overriding worries that might be bothering you.

2. *Rerun the events of your day.* Let the Holy Spirit guide you through what happened. You may want to segment the day and think it through like this: Start to coffee break, break to lunch, etc. Remember that the Spirit has the remote control. Let him call your attention to certain specifics.

3. *Respond to Christ's evaluation.* Get the "expert analysis" from Christ's Spirit. Take the time to listen for this. Then, in the space provided for that day, jot down what you sensed Christ telling you—what things were well done and what things you need to improve.

═══════════════

Extend Worship into the Work Week

*Too many of us have a huge gap
between our Sunday church experience
and our day-to-day work.
Jesus wants to be Lord of our whole lives
and our whole schedules.*

Week One:
Recording Progress

Bridge the Gap between Church and Work
(Details on page 13.)

To help bridge the church/work gap I completed assignment number _____ on _____(date). The experience taught me that _____

_____

_____

_____.

Delight Others by Giving Away
the Presents of Christ
(Details on page 18.)

This week I tried to delight others by giving the presents of Christ three times in the following ways:

1. On _____ I gave a present of _____

    to _____.

2. On _____ I gave a present of _____

    to _____.

3. On _____ I gave a present of _____

    to _____.

Bridging the Gap
Sunday, Day One

Christ wants to transform my daily work. Through today's Scripture, 1 Peter 2:11-12, he is saying to me specifically,

"_____, *in your work situation*
(my name)

_____

_____."

The woman looked old, withered beyond her years. How old was she? Thirty? Thirty-five? Who could tell? The only obvious fact was her grotesque, gnarled body. Straightening up was impossible for her. For eighteen torturous years she had suffered like this, and no one could do anything to help.

Then one day she heard about a young itinerant preacher with a gift for healing. Rumor had it he was to appear at the local synagogue that Sabbath. Could this be a chance to escape her prison of flesh? She didn't know, but instantly she determined to get to that holy place, no matter the cost. Any chance was better than none. And that is why this misshapen daughter of Abraham somehow shuffled and hobbled one morning to Sabbath services.

She was a latecomer, of course—it's hard to get anywhere on time when each step sends meteors of fire hurtling up your spine—so she took a place near the back. The pain overwhelmed her by now. She was just about to scold herself for acting on foolish hopes when it happened.

He had been watching. He spoke, and his words—words of power and authority—exploded in her ears like the words that had shaped the worlds:

"Woman, you are set free from your infirmity!"

Instantly her body obeyed. Gone was the crookedness. Gone was the pain. Delight burst from her heart and worked its way out to waving arms and dancing feet and loud, wild praise. Her friends gasped and shouted. Everyone began chattering and laughing in sheer, unexpected joy . . . everyone, that is, except the one person you would expect to be among the happiest.

Luke tells the story: "Indignant because Jesus had healed on the Sabbath, the synagogue ruler said to the people, 'There are six days for work. So come and be healed on those days, not on the Sabbath' " (Luke 13:14).

That's almost harder to imagine than the miracle, isn't it? But to this religious leader, Christ's healing smacked of work, and synagogue bylaws made it clear that no work was to be done on the Sabbath.

With a few choice words the Lord responded:

"You hypocrites! Doesn't each of you on the Sabbath untie his ox or donkey from the stall and lead it out to give it water? Then should not this woman, a daughter of Abraham, whom Satan has kept bound for eighteen long years, be set free on the Sabbath day from what bound her?" (vv. 15-16).

His antagonists blushed at the rebuke. "All his opponents were humiliated," Luke writes, "but the people were delighted with all the wonderful things he was doing" (v. 17).

In the mind of this religious leader, no work was to be done on the Sabbath. This day was special, separated from the emphasis of the other days. And in some ways he was absolutely right! These *were* distinct and different worlds, the world of work and the world of worship. This leader knew the six had a tendency to consume the one, and I would say his concern is legitimate for our day as well.

But we must also be careful that the gap between work and worship doesn't become so vast that in protecting the one day, we lose the other six days. Monday through Saturday belong to God just as much as does Sunday. In a real sense, they are sacred, too. *All* of life is infused with God's presence.

It is right that we fight for Sunday being special. But reclaiming it for Christ will be a hollow victory if his ministry through us becomes ineffectual Monday through Friday. This religious leader's efforts to protect Sabbath worship for his God showed he was far too ready to barter off work as second-rate.

The lesson here for us is simple: We must bridge the gap between church and work. We must not let the two become isolated worlds that never touch. We must keep Sunday special, but we must also learn to wear some of our "Sunday best" on Monday and Tuesday and throughout the rest of the week.

The Bible's very language teaches us this. Ben Patterson makes it clear in his excellent book *The Grand Essentials*. He writes:

> There is a wonderful and pregnant ambiguity in the Bible's words for work and worship: in both the Old and New Testaments the word for each is the same. In the Old Testament, the Hebrew word *abad* can be translated either way—work or worship. Likewise, in the New Testament, the same Greek word, *leitourgein,* can either be translated liturgy, as in a service of worship, or it can be translated in purely secular terms, as in service to the king or service in the army. Only the context determines which meaning should be selected by the translator.
>
> One word, two meanings. Or is there really just one? The dual use of the word suggests that faithful service to God is rendered no more in a church service than it is in a "work service"—if the work is done for God. In the Bible there is an indissoluble unity between worship and work, since both are forms of service to God. There is the service we render to God in our worship and there is the service we render to him in our work. The former is the liturgy of the sanctuary, the latter is the liturgy of the world.[1]

Hear me: As surely as Christ visited the synagogue as recorded in Luke 13, he also visits the work settings of his people today. Yes, his body has changed. He no longer is a young, thirty-year-old Jewish teacher. Christ's body in the world today is his people. It's you and I. On Sunday we are the body gathered. The rest of the week we are the body scattered.

27

It was tragic in Luke 13 for Christ to do a miracle and not have it appreciated. It would be even more tragic for Christ to be prevented from continuing his miracle work today because his body refused him that privilege.

But I don't believe that will be the case with us, especially in these next fifty days. I have a conviction that Christ will be thrilled with who we are and who we allow him to become; with how we worship him in church on Sunday and how we work on his behalf the rest of the week; with the liturgy of worship and the liturgy of work.

Make Sunday special, yes! But let's not forget about the rest of the week. There's far too much at stake.

D.M.

End-of-the-Day Replay

1. Remove distractions

2. Rerun the events of your day

3. Respond to Christ's evaluation

I sensed Christ said to me:

"This was well done: _____

_____

_____."

"Work harder on this: _____

_____

_____."

☐ I remembered to pray the Ultimate Authority Prayer today.

Captured by a
Great Vision

Monday, Day Two

Christ wants to transform my daily work. Through today's Scripture, Romans 12:1-2, he is saying to me specifically,

"_____, *in your work situation*
　　　　　　　　(my name)

_____

_____."

What is the kingdom of Christ like?

It's like treasure hidden in a field. When a man found it, he hid it again and in his joy went and sold all he had to buy that field.

Or it's like a merchant looking for fine pearls. When he found one of great value he went away and sold everything he had and bought it.

It's revolutionary, an alternative kingdom, a kingdom that fulfills all our longings. It's a kingdom where Christ reigns, where his word holds ultimate authority, where citizenship is open to all, even to common folk. It's a kingdom that is to profoundly impact the world.

And it's a kingdom we're invited to join.

Most saw Zacchaeus the tax collector as an opportunist, a cheat, a traitor, a snake. But Christ envisioned him as a transformed kingdom-enthusiast, and that's what he became.

How do you describe the daily work of a lady who's been divorced five times and is now living with a man to whom she is not married? She's hardly a homemaker. Is she a prostitute? I'm not sure. But whereas others ostracized her, Jesus sat down and talked with her beside an ancient well, transforming her into a great public relations person for his kingdom.

Fishing—now, that has to be a respectable trade. But it doesn't seem quite as exciting as it once did when you've been asked by the new King, "How would you like to fish for men?"

If you read through the Gospels with an eye on the daily work of the people, you'll be surprised at the variety of jobs mentioned. It's literally beggars to kings, with a lot in between—lawyers, soldiers, merchants, priests, laborers, servants, slaves, you name it. The kingdom vision powerfully touched all these settings of employment.

Down through the centuries of the church, at the best of times when revival was hot and when Christ was perceived again as very near, the workplace was always affected. The gap was closed between Sunday and Monday.

David Matthews saw what happened to the workplace when revival touched his part of the world at the beginning of this century. In his book, *I Saw the Welsh Revival*, Matthews describes what happened in Wales from 1904 to 1905.

> The conversation of the miners with each other had undergone a change also which was most apparent when they met at mealtime. Occasionally, as they talked of the revival meetings which they attended, their souls would be filled with praises and the old mine would resound with their splendid voices as they testified to the goodness of the Lord. No talk of the coming prize fight! Football was not so popular now. They would recount the names of famous Welsh preachers to whom they had listened in the past—great men, who had preached great sermons which had produced little effect upon their own moral characters. Nevertheless, these sermons were now being rehearsed with gusto and enthusiasm—they were living again in the memories of these newly saved miners.

> On one occasion, we were told the manager happened to "come around" a mine for inspection, as was the daily custom. These fine fellows were congregated around their food-boxes, lamps stuck in the timber, hilariously

comparing their new spiritual experiences. . . The change in their manner and speech was astonishing. One of them, touching his cap politely, ventured to ask permission to give his testimony. With trembling voice and tear-stained face, he rehearsed dramatically how the Holy Spirit had guided him to a revival meeting. . . On the spot, he was so stabbed with conviction that he shouted aloud—"yelled" was the word he used—for forgiveness, which he received instantaneously, although he couldn't give any detailed explanation of how it happened. His bright, glowing face gave undeniable proof that something marvelous had taken place in his life. He turned to his manager and asked, "Mr. Beynon, have you experienced this? Have you, sir, been saved?" The answer was pathetic.

"No, Tom, I certainly cannot say, like you, that I am saved. Although, as you know I've been a deacon of my church for twenty-five years, no one ever asked me this very important question until you did so just now." He spoke with a tremor in his voice. . . Then Tom answered his superior officer, "Mr. Beynon, listen to God's Word: 'Behold, now is the accepted time; Behold now is the day of salvation.' " There and then the rough miner, with his equally rough friends, knelt around their manager in fervent prayer and pointed him to Christ. On that very spot he was saved through the instrumentality of these simple men. That piece of earth became sacred to the official, to be remembered as the place where he surrendered to the claims of Christ.[2]

Here was the kingdom flag being run to the top of the pole, way down in a coal mine. Small work commitments, like the ones we're asking during this fifty-day adventure, are easy to make when we're captured by a great vision. It's no big deal to sell everything to buy a field if we know it contains buried treasure.

During these fifty days, don't just see the adventure disciplines involved. Don't get bogged down in the assignments. Be captured by the vision of Christ transforming *your* daily work, of him calling you to something better than what you've known to date, of him challenging you to be part of something marvelous that affects both worship and work. Let it be as though you have discovered a pearl of great price. What's an adventure, if there's no fortune to be found?

It's not necessary that you ask your superior today, as did the miner, "Sir, have you been saved?" But such a scene could be repeated time and again if we know revival. If we do, I guarantee the workplace will be affected. The Sunday-Monday gap will be bridged, for when our Lord draws near, he impacts people's daily work! You can count on it.

Can he count on you? And me? Common folk, sure, but touched by greatness because of the King and the kingdom we represent. Make your monarch proud of you today!

D.M.

End-of-the-Day Replay

1. Remove distractions

2. Rerun the events of your day

3. Respond to Christ's evaluation

I sensed Christ said to me:

"This was well done: _____

_____

_____."

"Work harder on this: _____

_____

_____."

☐ I am remembering this week to give away three of the presents of Christ and to record this information on page 24.

Zionese

Tuesday, Day Three

Christ wants to transform my daily work. Through today's Scripture, Hebrews 13:15-16, he is saying to me specifically,

"_____, *in your work situation*
(my name)

_____

_____."

I never hear profanity at the "Chapel of the Air" offices. To remember what it's like, I have to go way back to a summer factory job I had between college years in the late 1950s. I heard crude words then, lots of them, but it's been a long time.

My children, Melissa, Joel, and Jeremy, say they hear profanity in school all the time.

Then there's theft. My kids say that if they leave things out at school, there's a good chance they'll be stolen—books, clothes, certainly money.

Theft just doesn't happen at the "Chapel of the Air" offices.

You know what? Sometimes ministers are around Christians so much we forget what the real world is like. If we're not careful, we can start preaching sermons as though everybody has the luxury of being surrounded by believers.

Surveys about church services expose one common complaint: ministers (like me) plan sermons and programs as though no one hated anybody Monday through Friday. Or as though women in the pews were never bothered by on-the-job sexual harassment. Or as if racism was a thing of the past. Or as if dirty jokes had vanished from traveling salesmen's repertoires. Or as though no one in church struggled with greed, or lying, or getting even.

The problems addressed in church services are "pharisaism" or "legalism" or "gnosticism"—but not commercialism or unionism or sexism. It's almost as if members of the church who want to function properly need to learn to speak "Zionese" and think only about theology and singing hymns.

When life returns to the church, however, it's because there are people who have learned to talk the language and the concerns of the working people. Revival history tells us so.

I think of John Wesley, who preached to crowds in England numbering in the twenty or thirty thousands. In churches? No. Coliseums? Hardly. In the fields. In fact, "crowds" may be too polite a word. "Mobs" would be more appropriate. Nevertheless, Wesley thanked God for getting together what he called his congregation of "drunkards, swearers, and Sabbath-breakers."

Prize-winning historian Roland H. Bainton wrote in *The Church of Our Fathers*:

> When a mob was nearly on the point of killing Wesley and a short club had just missed his head, he began quietly to pray. Suddenly then the leader of the mob turned and said, "Sir, I will spend my life for you: follow me and not one soul here shall touch a hair of your head." They got out safely and that man became a leader of Methodism.
>
> In his eighty-fifth year, of visiting a certain town, he wrote: "The last time I was here, about forty years ago, I was taken prisoner by an immense mob, gaping and roaring like lions: but how is the tide turned! High and low now lined the street, from one end of the town to the other, out of stark love and kindness, gaping and staring as if the king were going by."[3]

I wonder . . . what if today's church sermons were preached outside in the fields? Would anyone listen? Perhaps we've gotten too heady for our own good.

Our Lord was a marvelous field preacher. His messages weren't well received in the synagogues, but the common folk in the fields heard him gladly. Part of the reason is that Jesus refused to debate the fine points of the law, the favorite pastime of the religious leaders of his day.

Christ didn't quote the famous and learned rabbis. He talked simple truths, relevant to the people. He often illustrated from the work of his listeners: "A farmer went out to sow his seed. . . ." "The kingdom of heaven is like a net that was let down into the lake and caught all kinds of fish. . . ." "A man planted a vineyard. He put a wall around it, and dug a pit for the winepress and built a watchtower. . . ."

If we're again to know revival, all of us must work at making the gospel relevant to working folk. Certainly, preachers need to. But we can't do this on our own. We're so removed from the world most of you know. We desperately need your input if we're going to speak to needs.

I have to be told that profanity is something my kids face at school, that they hear it so often they almost get used to it. I wouldn't know it if they didn't tell me. I'm not tempted to cheat. But if they are, because that's how other kids get their good grades, then I need to address that issue.

A pastor-friend told me that during the past Olympic Games he was shocked one Sunday as he walked from the platform to greet his people. There in the lobby his staff was holding big cards over their heads, each with a score from one to ten, Olympic style, judging his sermon.

I'm all for that! We preachers need to know what you're thinking. If we are to know revival, all in the church must work at making the gospel message relevant to working men and women.

It's important that you let your pastor know about your work-related problems. How's he going to know the struggles you have otherwise? Invite your pastor, or pastor's spouse, or a church leader, to visit your work setting. When you do that, he or she will know better how to minister to you.

Apply a sermon idea to your work setting, and let your pastor know what you did. Pastors need to know how their ideas translate into hands-on action in the workplace. Or ask someone at church to pray for you regarding a work-related concern.

It's going to take ideas like these, involving all in the church, if we expect to see the day when the Spirit of God moves among us in revival force.

The "Zionese" has to stop. Talking in language that doesn't touch the worlds you live in is worse than useless. It's harming the cause of Christ.

Will you pray with me?

"Lord Jesus, help us make our message understood by the man or woman or teen or child in the street, or in the school, the park, or the field. Help us to communicate even as you did. For the cause of the kingdom of Jesus I pray. Amen."

D.M.

End-of-the-Day Replay

1. Remove distractions

2. Rerun the events of your day

3. Respond to Christ's evaluation

I sensed Christ said to me:

"This was well done: _____

_____

_____."

"Work harder on this: _____

_____

_____."

☐ I remembered to pray the Ultimate Authority Prayer today.

Hypocrites
Wednesday, Day Four

Christ wants to transform my daily work. Through today's Scripture, Matthew 7:3-5, he is saying to me specifically,
"_____, *in your work situation*
(my name)

_____

_____. "

What happened wasn't that big of a deal, but for some reason I find myself reliving it time and again.

Late one Monday morning I was sitting in my car at a red light in the center of town, minding my own business. I must have waited a fraction of a second too long, because no sooner had the red light turned green than the horn from the car behind me began to blast away.

Now, whenever this happens, I confess that my instinctual response is to move m - u - c - h, m - u - c - h s - l - o - w - e - r than normal. My old nature says, "I refuse to be intimidated by such tactics." So that's what I did.

When I looked in the rearview mirror, what I saw was hard to believe. The driver was absolutely furious—red-faced, shaking his fist in the air, and shouting words I was glad I couldn't hear. Then I realized, *I know him! That's a key leader in our church!*

The week before, in fact, I had heard him speak at a business-men's prayer meeting. I quickly turned and got out of the way. He never knew it was me.

My reactions to this little encounter were mixed. At first I thought, *Oh, man, what a hot dog!* Then I began to laugh—something like, *Now I have some inside information I can use if I ever need to.* The longer I thought about it, though, the more I began to wonder, *Is this guy for real? Or is he just a lot of show? Is he one thing on Sunday when he's around church people—polite, quiet, serene, never raises his voice—"My, that was a good sermon, pastor"—but something else the rest of the week?*

From that point on, it was hard for me to look at this man without thinking about those emotion-packed five or six seconds.

This real-life incident highlights one of the major areas we're focusing on in this fifty-day spiritual adventure. As Christ transforms our daily work, I'm convinced there's going to be a growing consistency between our Sunday behavior and the way we carry on the rest of the week.

Let me quote a verse. Do you recognize it?

"Whether you eat or drink or whatever you do on the Lord's Day, do it all for the glory of God."

Oops! That's not what it says, is it? Paul tells us in 1 Corinthians 10, "Whether you eat or drink or whatever you do [not just on the Lord's Day but all week long] do it all [in a way that would please Jesus] for the glory of God."

Pleasing Jesus, regardless of the day of the week, must always be our bottom line. That's true for a welder, a businessman, or a homemaker. That's the priority concern for a teacher, an office worker, a hospital administrator, a farmer, a college student, a mechanic, a grade schooler, a teenager, or a retiree. Whenever you eat or drink or whatever you do for a living, do it all, every day, in a manner that pleases Christ.

Jesus frequently used a harsh term to label those whose behavior was inconsistent, who acted religiously on the Lord's day but then lived otherwise in their daily work. Note his words in Matthew 6 (emphasis mine):

> When you give to the needy, do not announce it with trumpets, as the *hypocrites* do in the synagogues and on the streets to be honored by men. . . . When you pray, do

not be like the *hypocrites*, for they love to pray standing in the synagogues and on the street corners to be seen by men.

Did you catch the word? Hard to miss, isn't it? *Hypocrites.* Seven different times in Matthew 23, Jesus declares, "Woe to you, teachers of the law and Pharisees, you *hypocrites!*" Then he gets specific. "You blind guides! Fools! You shut the kingdom of heaven in men's faces. You're full of greed and self-indulgence. You snakes! You brood of vipers!"

Jesus doesn't candy-coat his words. He can spot hypocrites in a moment.

I've always taken a lot of pleasure in those passages where Jesus blasts away at the hypocrites. There's a part of me applauding on the sidelines, yelling, "Give it to them, Jesus! They're all bums! They deserve it!"

But then, a passage like Matthew 7:3, 5 forces me to identify with those I would rather blast. "Why do you look at the speck of sawdust in your brother's eye and pay no attention to the plank in your own eye?" Jesus asks. "You hypocrite, first take the plank out of your own eye [before you worry about your brother]."

The truth is, I'm *not* just standing on the sidelines. There are pieces of hypocrisy in my life that make *me* one of *them*. Oh, I can feel pretty smug, sitting in my car, thinking, *What a jerk!* about that leader in my church. But what about me and my inconsistencies? Wasn't I the guy who took a little too much pleasure by moving at a snail's pace? What other discrepancies are there between my Sunday behavior and how I act during the rest of the week? It's a lot more comfortable to concentrate on the flaws of others than it is to acknowledge my own.

Please don't think I want you to do some heavy-duty introspection to discover your true, hypocritical self. I merely want to call us all to a renewed commitment to a life of consistency.

And how can we make certain it happens? The best insurance against hypocrisy is to consciously take Jesus with you to work.

Go ahead. Follow through on one of the ten assignments under Discipline One in each of the weeks to come, seven in all—seven specific ways to avoid the pitfalls of hypocrisy.

How does this help to avoid the pitfalls of hypocrisy? I can guarantee that if, for example, you're saying positive things about your church or your pastor on the job, you'll be much more careful to behave consistently.

My friends, recognizing the presence of Jesus in your daily work takes effort. But it's worth it. The effort produces consistent behavior. So stay at it!

S.B.

End-of-the-Day Replay

1. Remove distractions

2. Rerun the events of your day

3. Respond to Christ's evaluation

I sensed Christ said to me:

"This was well done: _____

_____

_____."

"Work harder on this: _____

_____

_____."

☐ I have given away at least one of the presents of Christ this week and have recorded the information on page 24.

The Questions God Asks
Thursday, Day Five

Christ wants to transform my daily work. Through today's

Scripture, Proverbs 16:5, 18-19, he is saying to me specifically,

"_____, *in your work situation*
          (my name)

_____

_____ ."

_____

Several months ago a friend asked a question that brought me up short. "Karen Mains," he asked, "what drives you?"

Driven? Me, driven? In our family, the word *driven* is usually associated with David. But then everyone who knows us knows what drives David—an urgent, God-given belief in national, spiritual renewal. Perhaps they just don't know what drives me.

I considered my friend's question, examined my soul, talked it over with my husband, attempted to be as honest as possible, and came to a surprising and satisfactory conclusion—one which I think I'll keep tucked away in my own family circle.

My friend's question was a good one, and it led me to some ultimate truth about myself. I'm glad someone took the time to ask it of me. I'm discovering that it's the questions others ask of me, more than the things they tell me, that have the most profound implications on my personal spiritual journey.

41

Socrates was a Greek philosopher and teacher who lived about 469 to 399 years before Christ. History has judged him to be one of the finest western thinkers of all time. Socrates believed that man's evil and wrong actions arose from ignorance and the failure to investigate why people act as they do. He's credited with saying, "The unexamined life is not worth living."

Socrates devoted himself to seeking goodness and truth. He developed what has become known as the Socratic method in which questions are asked, and the resulting discussion discloses the inadequacy of certain unstated assumptions.

The Socratic method—this questioning of what individuals assume they know—tends to expose men's ignorance. It shows that many things assumed to be true are false.

Peter Kreeft, a professor of philosophy at Boston College, wrote an InterVarsity Press book titled, *Socrates Meets Jesus: History's Great Questioner Confronts the Claims of Christ.* The author imposes the Socrates of ancient Athens on the campus of a major university, enrolling him in the divinity school. The whole book is a dialogue conducted in the Socratic method in which the classic philosopher is brought closer and closer to the reality of the truth about Christ. The book is a dramatic portrayal of reason used wisely in search of truth.

Being confronted with questions is often the way we discover truth about ourselves, about the universe, about spiritual realities.

Have you ever considered the questions that God asks?

From the beginning of time, God seems to use methods of teaching and learning that force his creatures to confront truth. He calls to Adam after the disobedience in Eden, "Where are you?" This is more than a demand for fallen man to reveal his hiding place. It's a question that forces Adam to reveal his sinful condition. God questions Eve, "What is this that you have done?"

God questions Abraham: "Where is Sarah, your wife?" This could be taken as a question about physical place; Sarah was actually hiding in the nether parts of the tent, doubting and giggling at the promises that she, an old woman and infertile, would birth an heir. But I think God's question was really aimed at examining Sarah's faith journey. "Where are you, Sarah? Do you still believe?"

The Scripture is filled with God's questions. To Elijah, after his tremendous spiritual victory at Mount Carmel and his subsequent flight after receiving Queen Jezebel's threats, God asks: "What are you doing *here*, Elijah?"

He asks Isaiah, "Whom shall I send, and who will go for us?"

The questioning of God goes on and on. "What do you mean?" "How do you say . . . ?" "What do you see?" In fact, the very ministry of Christ seems to hinge not only on proclamation of truth, but also on divine questions.

"Which is easier," he asked, "to say, 'Your sins are forgiven,' or 'Rise up and walk'?" "Can you make wedding guests fast while the bridegroom is with them?" "Is it lawful on the Sabbath to do good or harm?" "Where is your faith?" "What is your name?" "Who was it that touched me?" "Who do people say that I am?" "What is written in the law? How do you read?"

What if you, today, were to hear your Maker question you? How would you answer, "Where are you?" How would you answer, "What have you done? Why are you angry, and why has your countenance fallen?" How many times has *that* question forced me to consider myself? Once I come to the source of my anger, I often begin a journey toward radicalizing truth. Often I discover that I'm really angry with myself.

All of God's questions have profound impact, impact beyond their apparent, surface meaning. If we listen and respond, they have an impact that always brings us to radicalizing truth.

God's questions are for young and old. A question Christ asked Peter is for every child, woman, man, and aged person: "Do you love me more than these?"

In fact, the questions God asks can take an eternity to answer. Each one—"Where is your faith?" "What is your name?"—can profoundly shake our souls with the reality that we do not know the answers. We have to *find* the answers.

As I wrote this article, I realized I hadn't taken time to let God ask some of the questions he needed to ask of me. So I sat myself down, stilled myself, and said, "Lord, do you have anything you need to ask of me?" I heard his question speaking through the Scriptures I had read that day, through my quiet time of prayer, through the whispers of the Holy Spirit. God's questions are never simple! I'm still working on my answer.

You, too, may want to consider yourself. What does God want to ask of you today?

As you find a moment to sit in quiet or drive in the car, as you sit at your desk or take a half-hour for coffee, as you commute home from work or hold a child in your arms, in the few minutes of recess or the pause after the operation, ask this of God: "Are there any questions you need to ask me today?"

Then listen. You may be surprised at what you hear.

K.M.

End-of-the-Day Replay

1. Remove distractions

2. Rerun the events of your day

3. Respond to Christ's evaluation

I sensed Christ said to me:

"This was well done: _____

_____

_____."

"Work harder on this: _____

_____

_____."

☐ I have established a support relationship with another Christian and am meeting at least once a week.

Picky, Picky, Picky
Friday, Day Six

Christ wants to transform my daily work. Through today's Scripture, Philippians 4:8, he is saying to me specifically,

"_____, *in your work situation*
(my name)

_____

_____. "

I've had several types of daily work since I became the owner of a Social Security card. Some I was suited for, others I wasn't.

My first job was as a dining-hall waitress in a nursing home. I enjoyed the older folks, particularly the women. They talked with me, encouraged me to take a moment and sing to them when the organ was played at supper time, watched for my dates to pick me up, and gave me their considerable evaluation of the young man the next day. I was their "darling," and they became the bright spots in a job I learned to think of as drudgery.

In fact, between my disinterest in my assigned work—serving supper, then scraping and carting away mounds of dirty dishes and garbage—and their encouragement of my social life, I was nearly fired.

I was responsible to Mrs. C, a woman whose primary objective seemed to be to get home as early as possible every night. She watched the teenage help like a hawk, circling the dining hall looking for any *faux pas*.

"Ah-HA! *Another* butter-pat paper in the food garbage! How many times do I have to tell you, SEPARATE the garbage!"

It was enough to make me want to hang up my hair net and blue smock and walk away. Oh, the constant nagging evaluation of that poor woman! I think the day I quit was the only time I saw her smile.

I've grown up since those days and I've learned how important feedback is in our daily work. I'm much more open to the suggestions of the "Mrs. Cs" than I used to be. In fact, in my present daily work, I'm *dependent* on feedback. While I'm working behind a microphone in the studio, I'm dependent upon other people to help me through their feedback.

If I should make the tiniest mistake, s-s-stutter a little, I'll be interrupted by a voice that sounds a lot like David Mains telling me to "Try it again, Valerie. It wasn't quite clear." Or if I fail to enunciate: "Valerie, the word isn't 'ta,' it's 'to.' 'To enunciate.' " Right. Or move a fraction of an inch from the pattern of the microphone: "This is Barbara, the engineer. Valerie, you're off mike." OK, OK!

Now I have two choices: Throw my hands in the air and declare, "Picky, picky, *picky!*"; or take my co-workers' advice, trust them, and let them help me communicate as well as I can.

In much the same way, let's be honest and admit that being aware of the Lord's presence in our daily work can produce the same irritation. While we enjoy the comfort we receive from sensing him with us, there are times when his still, small voice is maddeningly correct—sensitizing us to character faults we would rather ignore, repeating our own words that sound rude or obnoxious when heard later in the quiet of our hearts, or asking us to go back to someone and apologize.

Sometimes we may feel like not listening, throwing our hands in the air and shouting, "Picky, picky, *picky!*" That's exactly what many believers do. But by ignoring his feedback, they begin a process of desensitization that ultimately ends in disaster.

One of the earliest accounts in the Bible about man and his daily work is also an account of man's struggle with this still, small voice of the Lord. Cain, a farmer, the firstborn son of Adam and Eve, brought a portion of his crops to the Lord for an offering. His younger brother, Abel, a shepherd, also made a sacrifice from his daily work. Scripture tells us that the Lord accepted Abel's offering, but not Cain's. This was too much for Cain. We're told his face grew dark with fury, and we can almost imagine him saying, "Picky, picky, *picky!*"

The Lord had some feedback for Cain. He questioned him: "Why are you angry? Why is your face so dark with rage?" Then the Lord offered him a more pleasant possibility: "It can be bright with joy if you will do what you should! But if you refuse to obey, watch out. Sin waits to attack you, longing to destroy you." And then this hopeful word: "But you can conquer it" (Genesis 4:6-7, TLB).

You know the story, don't you? Cain feels rejected instead of instructed. He doesn't conquer his sin, but instead kills his brother. The Lord banishes him from the land and he becomes a fugitive. And that's not all. There's an important statement that follows. Scripture says, "So Cain went out from the presence of the Lord."

Cain would never again listen to the Lord's annoying, still, small voice. He was too hardened to hear the gentle reminder to watch for sin, and he would reap the self-destruction of his anger and hatred. With no warning voice ringing in his conscience, Cain's better self was subjected to his worse self—*and God's voice fell on a deaf soul*. It was true he would never again be irritated into shouting, "Picky, picky, *picky!*" But it was equally true he would never again feel the comfort of fellowship with his gracious God.

Scholars have often debated about the identifying mark that the Lord put on Cain as a warning not to kill him. I suspect that the father of murderers could have been picked out of a crowd even without an identifying mark. Cain's toughened face told a story of the departure of everything holy and good, the prototype of every unrepentant criminal. As people looked at him, they knew he was a man totally divorced from God.

Proverbs says that a wise man is glad to be instructed, but a self-sufficient man falls flat on his face. A wise man or woman recognizes that enjoying God's presence also means giving God permission to be "picky, picky, *picky.*"

At the end of the day, it is always wonderful to hear the words, "Well done, my servant!" But when it's that insistent voice we hear, "Watch out! Sin is waiting to attack you," how will we respond? Will you or I think, "Picky, picky, *picky,*" harden our

47

hearts and desensitize ourselves to his presence? Or will we be eager learners, receptive listeners?

We must learn to accept not only the comfort of his presence, but his feedback on how we're living. So keep doing that End-of-the-Day Replay. And I promise you, you'll appreciate not only his presence, but his insistent, still, small voice as well.

V.B.

End-of-the-Day Replay

1. Remove distractions

2. Rerun the events of your day

3. Respond to Christ's evaluation

I sensed Christ said to me:

"This was well done: _____

_____

_____."

"Work harder on this: _____

_____

_____."

☐ This week I gave away three presents of Christ and recorded this information on page 24.

Growing Strong Fast
Saturday, Day Seven

Christ wants to transform my daily work. Through today's
Scripture, Exodus 31:12-15, he is saying to me specifically,

"_____, *in your work situation*
　　　　　(my name)

_____

_____."

━━━
━━━

DAVID: Karen, do you remember that scripture in Hebrews 12 which asks, "For what son is there whom his father does not train and correct and discipline?" (Amplified).

KAREN: David, I have a very interesting relationship with that scripture. Whenever I'm feeling sorry for myself, I mean really maudlin and pitiful, I'll flip through the Scripture and say, "Oh, Lord, you have to encourage me today!" Invariably I'll get this passage, and particularly verse 12: "So then, brace up and reinvigorate and set right your slackened and weakened and drooping hands, and strengthen your feeble and palsied and tottering knees" (Amplified). The Lord says to me, "Brace up! Get on with it, Mains!"—especially in verse 6: "For the Lord corrects and disciplines every one whom He loves" (Amplified).

DAVID: That's a wonderful passage; it's exactly what you need!

KAREN: How about you? Did your parents ever correct you?

DAVID: Mom always corrected me in the area of grammar. If I said things incorrectly in a sermon, no matter what happened—fifty people could come forward—she would correct me. And I appreciated that. "David," she would say, "don't mix the singular and plural pronouns! Don't say, 'If someone wants an adventure journal, we'll see that they get it on time.' No, David, say, 'If someone wants an adventure journal, we'll see to it that that person gets it on time.' But don't change from singular to plural!" She continues to this day. Because of Mom I speak much weller than I used to!

KAREN: My mother used to poke me in the back and say, "Stand up straight, Karen; don't slouch." How I wish she were around to say those things to me now, because I find myself slouching when I get tired.

DAVID: "Clean your room!" Did you ever hear your mother say that to you?

KAREN: I think it's a universal parental statement.

DAVID: You say it to Jeremy all the time.

KAREN: I have been saying it to him for four years. And he still has yet to clean his room. It seems he gets a third of the way in and that's it.

DAVID: And it's always the same third! The other two-thirds have never been cleaned. How about teachers, Karen? I appreciate the teachers who disciplined me, who said, "You're not going to get by with this, David. This is something you *must* learn." They weren't mean, they were just tough. They wouldn't let me slack off. I had to do it right.

KAREN: I had an English teacher my senior year in high school who was like that. She shifted my thinking. She insisted that any report or paper we did had to be generated out of a thinking process. She asked questions, she challenged our presuppositions. I believe she nicely kicked me into a thinking posture. I've been grateful to her for years.

DAVID: Karen, have you ever had a boss who disciplined you and said, "You have to get this right"?

KAREN: Yes, an editor. One of the very first editors I had—in fact, the woman who started me in writing—often would send work back and say, "You can do better than this, Karen." It was hard to get those ideas together and to submit them in the midst of having four small children and being a pastor's wife. She made me angry! I would fuss and stew around, until I determined I was going to show her. Then I would turn in something that was much, much better than my first effort. I'm very grateful she didn't let me settle for cheap work.

DAVID: The person who holds up the high standard is the one who brings you along in the way you want to develop. That's the way Jesus is. I believe one reason we don't see revival in the church is that Christ's standard isn't held up high enough. Jesus does hold up a good standard; he isn't a mean teacher, but he does discipline us and keep us moving along in the spiritual life. The strongest spiritual sons and daughters are those who willingly submit to this training program of Christ's. What do you think would be the opposite of this?

KAREN: It would be to ignore it or to despise it or to settle for a low standard.

DAVID: But who likes spiritual discipline? I don't.

KAREN: No one does. Scripture knows that. Hebrews 12:10, 11 says, ". . . But God disciplines us for our good, that we may share in his holiness. No discipline seems pleasant at the time. . . ."

DAVID: The big question is *how* to do this. How does one learn to receive the discipline of Jesus?

KAREN: It's kind of paradoxical, isn't it? In his love, God is always disciplining us and correcting us so that we will achieve his high standard ("that we may become sharers in his own holiness . . ."). But we have to enter into the discipline process with him. We have to be willing, we almost have to "give him permission." We have to say to him, "I want you to do this so that I can become everything you expect me to be. I want you to correct me so that I can use and develop the gifts you have given me."

Recently I had an upsetting conversation with a friend. We just didn't seem to understand one another. I came home from that encounter huffing and puffing, concluding that my friend had a superiority complex, that he felt greater than me in every way. I was mad. But as I looked at this incident, it was interesting how the Holy Spirit said in that loud whisper of his, "And do you not feel superior yourself to some people in some way?"

That word of correction prompted me to examine myself. It was a good journey for me to take, because I discovered some atti-

51

tudes of superiority concerning my gifts and abilities that I needed to correct. I had to ask the Lord to forgive me. Without my willing cooperation, without my wanting God to correct me, I probably would have just gone on being mad at my friend.

DAVID: The important thing is that you took the time to allow God to speak with you. When any of us does that, I believe we'll find he is a wonderful friend, a Father in the true sense of the word. He is a good teacher, a wise boss.

So, good friends, don't tell God that you'll get by on your own in your spiritual walk, that you don't need him. Submit to his correction. More than that, initiate times when he can speak with you in the quiet of time alone together. It will be worth your while and you will grow strong quickly! And isn't that what spiritual adventures are all about?

D.M., K.M.

End-of-the-Day Replay

1. Remove distractions

2. Rerun the events of your day

3. Respond to Christ's evaluation

I sensed Christ said to me:

"This was well done: _____

_____

_____."

"Work harder on this: _____

_____

_____."

☐ I remembered to pray the Ultimate Authority Prayer today.

Week One Notes

1. Ben Patterson, *The Grand Essentials* (Waco, Tex: Word Books, 1987), pp. 76-77.

2. David Matthews, *I Saw the Welsh Revival* (Chicago: Moody Press, 1951), pp. 57-58..

3. Roland H. Bainton, *The Church of Our Fathers* (New York: Charles Scribner's Sons, 1941), pp. 192-193.

Become Sensitive to the Spirit's Input

*Jesus promised to send
a Counselor to guide us
and to remind us of his teaching.*

Week Two:
Recording Progress

Bridge the Gap between Church and Work
(Details on page 13.)

To help bridge the church/work gap I completed assignment num-

ber _____ on _____(date). The experience taught

me that _____

_____

_____

_____.

*Delight Others by Giving Away
the Presents of Christ*
(Details on page 18.)

This week I tried to delight others by giving the presents of Christ
three times in the following ways:

1. On _____ I gave a present of _____

   to _____.

2. On _____ I gave a present of _____

   to _____.

3. On _____ I gave a present of _____

   to _____.

Everyone Needs
a Little Help
Sunday, Day Eight

Christ wants to transform my daily work. Through today's

Scripture, Galatians 5:16-26, he is saying to me specifically,

"_____, *in your work situation*

_____

_____ ."

Without some help along the way, it would be extremely difficult to become concertmaster of a great orchestra, rise to the presidency of a Fortune 500 company, or win a Nobel prize. I suppose it's possible, but without a little help here and there, it wouldn't be easy.

Similarly, it would be next to impossible, without assistance, to become . . . godly!

Now, one way to fool people in church is to keep your humanity hidden. You can sit alone, look pious on Sundays, and avoid getting involved. Even then it would be hard! Attempt the same silent approach in your work setting, and people might say you're introverted—but I'm not sure they would declare you godly. Being thought of as a saint is harder to achieve than that.

Learning to live for the Lord is *difficult.* And the way to go about it is not with a "do-it-thyself" kit.

Fortunately, the Lord has provided for us the very best of teachers. Name the qualities you'd want in a perfect teacher—patience, wisdom, experience, fairness, concern—and this instructor exemplifies them all. Jesus told his disciples about him.

Although the twelve had been instructed by our Lord himself, Jesus said in John 16 that it was to their advantage that he go away. Otherwise the Counselor, their new Helper, the Teacher of spiritual things, couldn't come to them.

In Galatians 5:16-26, we are instructed to *live* by this Spirit, and *to be led* by this Spirit, and to *keep in step* with this Spirit. The big question is *how.*

In Acts 24:16, the apostle Paul says, "So I always take pains to have a clear conscience toward God and toward men" (RSV). To Timothy he writes, "I serve God with a clear conscience." The conscience is one of the ways by which Christ instructs us through his Spirit.

Prior to conversion, the conscience is programmed by the norms of the society in which you are reared. But upon becoming a member of Christ's kingdom, his Spirit takes over this facet of your instruction.

It's almost like an alarm goes off in the back of your head whenever you step out of God's guidelines as found in his word. Now, it's not a literal alarm—BZZZZT!—but it's just as real.

Let's suppose that at work you begin to gossip about somebody you don't like. Usually it isn't very long until your conscience triggers that alarm. BZZZZT! Then you have a choice: You either say to your indwelling Teacher, "Thank you for this correction," or you shut off the alarm and treat it like an unwelcome clock at the beginning of the day. "I'm enjoying what I'm doing," you say, "don't bother me now!"

Sad to say, too many Christians have become adept at silencing the work of the Spirit in their conscience. What results is them having to program the conscience on their own, something for which they're unequipped.

"But how do I know it's the Holy Spirit and not the devil?" someone asks. "Can't he put thoughts in my mind also?"

I'm sure he can. But usually it's not that hard to tell the difference. That passage in Galatians goes on to say that "the acts of the sinful nature are obvious." When the Holy Spirit, who indwells us on Christ's behalf, confronts us, it's not that hard to figure out if the message is from him or the devil. It's pretty obvious.

Sometimes we won't allow God to work unless he makes his activities so up-front that there's no possible way to deny it's his voice. "If he would just speak aloud," we say, "it would resolve a lot of problems." But how would you like God to say your name aloud and then, "Stop thinking lustful thoughts!!" You would be humiliated. Why, then, deny the Holy Spirit an opportunity to graciously get your attention through your conscience?

David McKenna, the president of Asbury Seminary, has told about a troubled soul who went for professional help. "What's your problem?" the counselor queried. "Well, you see, I don't have the willpower to resist temptation and my conscience is uneasy!" "And you'd like to strengthen your willpower, is that right?" The patient dropped his head and answered sheepishly, "Not exactly. If it's alright with you, sir, I'd prefer to have my conscience weakened."

It's possible that through the years you've followed an unstated policy of trying to get accustomed to a troubled conscience. It's affected how you pray, because of lies you've told or the knowledge that you've cheated at work or at school. How difficult it is to tell others what Christ is doing in your life if you have to wonder whether they've heard how you wronged an employee or an employer!

Learn to be sensitive to Christ's use of your conscience. Know that if you refuse him access, you have the impossible job of trying to become godly without his divine help.

That the Spirit is a wonderful teacher can't be denied. But the question is, what about his pupils? Let me ask you, what qualities do you think a first-rate teacher would look for in an outstanding student?

"I imagine respect would be important," you say, "maybe punctuality in carrying out assignments. There should be an attitude of going beyond what's expected, things like that!"

Good. That's a start!

I'm suggesting that all of us develop into really fine pupils of the Holy Spirit. I would like our relationship to God's divinely assigned Teacher to demonstrate the high qualities expected of any good student. Let us show respect for this best of all instructors. We're not to look the other way when he's trying to teach us something, or make lame excuses when he wants our attention, or fail to do what he requests at the time he expects it. Let's get beyond doing only what is absolutely necessary to get by. Go out of your way to please your Teacher and you'll quickly become more Christlike, more godly.

Give the Spirit the privilege of having an honor roll student under his wing! You'll be amazed at how exciting it will make your Christian walk. You . . . and your Teacher. What a team!

D.M.

End-of-the-Day Replay

1. Remove distractions

2. Rerun the events of your day

3. Respond to Christ's evaluation

I sensed Christ said to me:

"This was well done: _____

_____

_____."

"Work harder on this: _____

_____

_____."

☐ To bridge the church/work gap I have completed one of the weekly assignments and recorded this information on page 56.

Seeing Christ
Monday, Day Nine

*Christ wants to transform my daily work. Through today's
Scripture, 1 John 3:18-24, he is saying to me specifically,
"_____, in your work situation*

_____

_____ *."*

Have you ever met someone who claimed to have seen the
Lord?

I've never literally seen the Lord, but on occasion someone
will tell me he or she has—like one man I spoke with the other
day.

He had been close to death, and told me that one evening
Christ came to his hospital room and stood quietly at the foot of
his bed for some time. The experience was very real to him, and I
don't feel compelled to decide whether it happened.

I believe I'm good at seeing Christ through eyes of faith, the
way people do during times of revival. The outstanding character-
istic of genuine revival is an overwhelming sense of the presence of
the Lord. That's the reason for the title of a book I've written on
this topic, called *The Sense of His Presence*. Let me underscore this
point: During revival, people sense that God is very near.

The following quote is from a book titled *Fire in the Church,* by Ted Rendall, president of Prairie Bible Institute in Three Hills, Alberta, Canada. He writes,

> During a spiritual awakening, there is, first, an overwhelming awareness of the presence of God among His people.
>
> "What have been the outstanding features of this movement?" asked Duncan Campbell of the Lewis revival of the years 1949-53. "First, an awareness of God," and then he went on to say, "I have no hesitation in saying that this awareness of God is the crying need of the church today."[1]

I say "amen" to that! In the book *The Rain From Heaven,* Arthur Wallace writes, "In times of revival, a man is not only made conscious that God is there, but often it will seem to him that he is there to deal with him alone." Revival is always marked by this intense insight that God has come near—sometimes uncomfortably near, and other times delightfully near, depending on the spiritual state of the person.

To see Christ the way people do during revival, we must make every effort to be holy. Let me say it again: *To see Christ the way people do during revival, we must make every effort to be holy.*

That's because there are certain things that just don't go together. Fire and water, for example. They don't mix. Or light and darkness, love and hate. We are told repeatedly that drinking and driving don't go together. Put this on your list as well: sinning and seeing God. If you choose sin, forget about seeing God through eyes of faith.

I'm not saying you can't be a Christian, but I am saying that you jettison the privilege of drawing delightfully close to the Lord when you say, "Yes, I want to draw close to the Lord, but I also want to hold on to a pet sin or two."

Hebrews 12:14 reads, "Make every effort . . . to be holy; without holiness no one will see the Lord."

This is a good lesson to learn early on. Sin and seeing God don't go together. With great effort, even cats and dogs might learn to live together, but God—because he by his very nature is holy—can't get used to sin.

When you sin, it's just like Adam and Eve—you want to hide from God. Without being told, you know he's holy. Your sin makes you feel uncomfortable if he's around.

But when you're tempted to sin and you purposely say, "No, I'm not going to do this," it's like God draws very close. Sometimes it's a long battle before the temptation goes away, but when you eventually win, you know his delightful presence. You feel his pleasure. And you see him through eyes of faith. There is great pleasure in overcoming temptation.

In a sense, this spiritual adventure is designed to let you get a touch of what this is all like. It lets you taste what revival is all about. We're trying to help you to sense the presence of the Lord in your daily work, to know the unique joy of seeing him there by faith.

If you like what you've experienced so far, believe me, you'll like revival even more! But remember, sensing Christ by faith is not the same as make-believe. Jesus is truly present through his Holy Spirit. Did you catch the word? "Holy." So don't be surprised if he challenges you on a matter of holiness.

Regularly doing the End-of-the-Day Replay keeps you from long-standing sin. As you learn each night from the Holy Spirit, you get better at seeing God through eyes of faith. And that draws you closer to experiencing spiritual revival. That's not make-believe, either.

A man recently called on me regarding business. When our conversation was through, he told me he had been a student at Asbury during the revival of 1970. It had marked his life and he would never be the same. "Some people took off their shoes when they entered the chapel because it was holy ground," he said.

The book *One Divine Moment*, edited by Robert Coleman, gives a sense of that extraordinary time.

> For 185 hours—without any interruption—the services had continued! . . . most of the students on the campus of the college and seminary knelt at the altar, and there were thousands of other persons who made a similar dedication. The whole spiritual tone of the campus was completely changed.
>
> Even now, months later, a few people gather each evening to pray, witness, and rejoice together. Also during most hours of the day someone may be seen

entering the chapel. They kneel to pray for a few minutes, then leave. Others just sit and stare at the altar so rife with precious memories. If one looks closely, tears may be seen coursing down their cheeks.

Perhaps those tears express more eloquently than words what has happened. There is no human vocabulary that can capture the full dimension of one divine moment. In some ways, it seems almost like a dream—yet it happened. We saw it with our eyes. In a way impossible to describe, God was in our midst. Those of us who were there can never look upon the things of this world quite the same.[2]

Friends, such an experience *can* be ours. God's Spirit may move so powerfully upon us, too. But we must be holy . . . both in church and in the workplace. That part is up to us.

D.M.

End-of-the-Day Replay

1. Remove distractions

2. Rerun the events of your day

3. Respond to Christ's evaluation

I sensed Christ said to me:

"This was well done: _____

_____

_____."

"Work harder on this: _____

_____

_____."

☐ I am remembering this week to give away three of the presents of Christ and to record this information on page 56.

Not a Bargain
Tuesday, Day Ten

Christ wants to transform my daily work. Through today's Scripture, 1 Peter 2:11-12, he is saying to me specifically,
"_____, *in your work situation*
_____
_____. "

═══

One hundred fifty billion dollars a year. That's how much it's estimated the "blue flu" costs American employers. The "blue flu" is people calling in sick when they're really not.

Another almost equally huge sum—one hundred to one hundred fifty billion dollars yearly—is lost through excessive coffee breaks, longer-than-should-be lunches, and people who get to work late.

The research company that published these figures states that employees who engage in time theft are more likely also to steal merchandise from their employers.

I don't care whose work is being referred to, dishonesty, theft, sin costs everybody plenty. How much money do you think could be saved in the workplace if sin could just be voluntarily set aside? Just imagine—when you take a plane ride, all the expense of checking passengers for weapons wouldn't be necessary. How wonderful if the savings could be passed on to the customer!

We could do away with locks in homes and offices and cars, on bikes and lockers. We wouldn't need nearly as many police or judges or lawyers. Who said "ministers"? You're probably right! With sin no longer so popular, what would we ministers have to talk about?

I can name a lot more savings we'd know if we could just say no to sin. What's on your list? Whatever you come up with, I guarantee you that we would come out better in terms of lower prices, more replacement jobs, and a better life for all. That's because sin is never the bargain we think it is.

A recent movie called *The House of Games* is about an author/psychologist who gets caught up with some con men who teach her the tricks of the trade. She's fascinated by it all and loves the excitement. What she doesn't know soon enough is that she is the intended victim.

Isn't that where our society is?

Oh, we love our sin—it's fascinating and exciting—but what we don't realize is that we're the ones paying an incredibly high price for it. And what's true about the work world is also true regarding the world of each individual worker. Sin is always overpriced. You know that already regarding other people's sin, don't you? Especially the obvious ones: the factory supervisor who's an alcoholic; that halfway attractive gal at the office who gets what she wants by giving out sexual favors; the retiree who lies about his supposed accomplishments; the student who cheats; the businessperson whose bottom line is greed.

In each case, you have no doubt but what these people pay far more for their sin than it's worth. But did you know that this is also true regarding your smaller and less obvious sin?

I'm not just asking on a true/false quiz, "Would you mark this statement as true: 'All sin costs more than it's worth'?" I know what you would say. But in the way you live, does what you know have a bearing on how you do your work? Is it true in practice that for even the small dishonesty, you're aware that you might have to give up the confident witness you had for Christ?

For limited lust (only in your mind), it could mean you'll lose your excitement about church. It bothered you recently to hear a Sunday service begin, "Almighty God, to you all hearts are open, all desires known, and from you no secrets are hid." You heard the words and the Spirit pricked your conscience, but you weren't ready to give up the forbidden thoughts. Strange. And now it seems your interest in church isn't as keen. Oh, what a high price to pay for a sexual fantasy!

Or maybe you got disgusted with someone at work and refused to forgive and extend love for Christ's sake. The thought of giving that person an adventure present of love—Christ's love—actually turns you off to these fifty days. How sad!

To miss out because of such a small thing . . . but it's consistent with sin being expensive.

The truth is that everyone who works hard for a living needs to be reminded that sin is way overpriced. A good paycheck is hard to come by. Because it is, nobody wants to get ripped off.

The same is true regarding spiritual pay. You have to fight hard for certain benefits of walking with Christ. Why blow them? What sin pays, in a working person's language, is found in Romans chapter 6: "The wages of sin is death." That means being cut off from God. So the payoff of sin is to be cut off from nearness to God. Does that sound like a good deal to you? Then don't be ignorant or forgetful of this basic fact of life. All those who work hard for a living should be reminded that sin is priced too high.

Here's that same truth in another scripture, Proverbs 11:19: "He who pursues evil goes to his death." Interestingly, both these verses give the reverse side as "life" or "oneness with God." What an attractive quality! It's something we want to know more of during these fifty days.

Here's the first half of Proverbs 11:19: "The truly righteous man attains life." Righteous here means the one who does what's right in God's sight.

So now the big question. How do we learn to do what's right in God's sight and attain life?

A practical adventure suggestion is to make it a habit each evening to do the End-of-the-Day Replay. Determine to be obedient to Christ's evaluation of each day. That will put you in a place where life or closeness to God marks your friendship. Romans 6:23: "The wages of sin is death, but the gift of God is eternal life in Christ Jesus our lord."

Hear me. There is nothing better in all the world than close-ness to the Lord. That's life! For now and for eternity. If the world were close to God it really would be much better off. Its closeness to the devil is costing dearly. Remember? And that's true for us, as well. For you and for me.

We don't want to forget.

D.M.

End-of-the-Day Replay

1. Remove distractions

2. Rerun the events of your day

3. Respond to Christ's evaluation

I sensed Christ said to me:

"This was well done: _____

_____

_____."

"Work harder on this: _____

_____

_____."

☐ I remembered to pray the Ultimate Authority Prayer today.

The Anti-Scrooge Meter
Wednesday, Day Eleven

Christ wants to transform my daily work. Through today's Scripture, Ecclesiastes 3:13, he is saying to me specifically,
"_____, *in your work situation*

_____

_____."

How would you like to work for Ebenezer Scrooge?

In the classic *A Christmas Carol* by Charles Dickens, Ebenezer Scrooge was a difficult taskmaster. He made no bones about it that his bottom line was to make a shilling, and in the process to spend as little as possible. Old Scrooge was so cheap that even in bitter cold weather he would have just a small fire in his bleak, counting-house office.

His only employee, Bob Cratchet, was allowed an even smaller fire. As the time approached on Christmas eve to close the office, Scrooge's nephew stopped by to wish him a Merry Christmas. His response? A sneer. Scrooge hated sentiment. The only thing that mattered to him was money. To him, Christmas was a time when people spent more than they should and found themselves a year older and no richer.

Begrudgingly, Scrooge did allow his clerk to have Christmas Day off. That was the only concession he made to the holiday. Still, he told Cratchet, "Make sure you're at work all the earlier the day after Christmas!"

So again I ask, how would you like to work for Ebenezer Scrooge?

Perhaps someone's thinking, "Since you brought it up, I think I *do* work for Ebenezer Scrooge. There's no question that my boss's bottom line is the buck. The motto he lives by is, 'Task first. People are expendable.' No matter what, he never seems satisfied. He's always trying to get more out of me—more productivity, more and more responsibilities. But, of course, no more pay. Not only is my job devoid of praise, I *never* get a raise. And now that you've got me thinking about it, my boss doesn't like it when I take days off, either. He works seven days a week and thinks everyone else should, too."

Maybe you don't work *for* a Scrooge type, but you're absolutely certain you work *with* one. A co-worker's very presence seems to pollute the atmosphere in your place of work. Never gets a headache, only gives them. You're positive this person's mission in life is to make everyone else miserable. The negativism. The insensitivity. The selfishness. It's almost intolerable.

My concern today isn't whether you work for or with a Scrooge type. The truth is, it's almost impossible to be in the work force without encountering such people along the way. That being the case, what really concerns me is, what are *you* bringing to the job? The qualities of a Scrooge? Or those of a Bob Cratchet?

How much of a Bob Cratchet is there spilling over from you? Good spirited? Grateful? Patient? Uncritical?

In spite of how much we may detest Scrooge-like behavior, I'm convinced there's a little bit of Scrooge in each of us. Left on our own, these Scrooge-like tendencies are bound to intensify.

Be honest. Is your bottom line on the job often just a dollar? Are you so intent on getting the job done, so typically Mr. Productive, that you ignore the needs of your fellow workers?

Who of us hasn't fallen short in these areas? Without some kind of check and balance system, I'm afraid most of us, over the long haul, would become more Scrooge-like than we'd care to admit.

I believe God has graciously built into each of his children a check-and-balance system that I like to think of as an anti-Scrooge meter. He's provided his warm and loving self in the person of His Spirit who walks beside us and lives within us. The Lord tells us through Galatians 5:16 to live by the Spirit, so we won't gratify the desires of our sinful (or Scrooge-like) selves. Then in verses 24-25 Paul says, "Those who belong to Christ Jesus have crucified [these sinful tendencies]. Since we live by the Spirit, let us keep in step with the Spirit."

The key to the check-and-balance system God provides us is to keep in step with the Spirit. Learning how to do this is one of the disciplines we've included in this adventure.

I really believe Christ can transform our daily work. Jesus wants to help us live consistently as Christians on the job—in the business world, the home, a school setting, wherever. For this to happen requires keeping in step with the Spirit.

It's intriguing that by the end of the story, old, miserly Ebenezer Scrooge underwent a total transformation. The hard-nosed, self-centered taskmaster became a kindhearted, generous benefactor, concerned about the welfare of everyone within his reach. And Scrooge never reverted to his old ways. He raised Bob Cratchet's salary, improved conditions in his office, contributed to charities, and became a second father to Cratchet's ailing son, Tiny Tim.

What was it that sparked Scrooge's reformation? As the story goes, it happened overnight.

One Christmas eve, Scrooge saw his whole life replayed before his eyes. He encountered the spirits of Christmas past, present, and future. It was this fresh perspective that motivated him to become a sterling example of sharing the joy of Christmas with his fellow man.

Unlike Scrooge's reform, the kind of transformation I'm urging for us isn't going to happen overnight. His experience is delightful storybook stuff, but this adventure is for real. For Christ to transform our daily work we must get in touch and keep in step with God's Holy Spirit.

Completing the End-of-the-Day Replay day in and day out for the remaining thirty-nine days of this adventure is one sure way to help you keep in step with God's Spirit. And best of all, I predict the results of this exercise will make a positive difference in your daily work.

It's something like this: Because of the Spirit, the old Scrooge is gone, and the transformed Scrooge is here to stay.

S.B.

End-of-the-Day Replay

1. Remove distractions

2. Rerun the events of your day

3. Respond to Christ's evaluation

I sensed Christ said to me:

"This was well done: _____

_____

_____."

"Work harder on this: _____

_____

_____."

☐ I have given away at least one of the presents of Christ this week and have recorded this information on page 56.

Think Small
Thursday, Day Twelve

Christ wants to transform my daily work. Through today's
Scripture, Proverbs 31:10-31, he is saying to me specifically,
"_____, *in your work situation*

_____

_____."

The book *Working*, by Studs Terkel, is an edited transcript of
people talking about what they do and their feelings about it. The
author interviewed the farmer and his wife, the miner, the heavy-
equipment operator, the receptionist, the airline stewardess, the
executive secretary, the sanitation truck driver, the washroom
attendant, the factory mechanic, the policeman, the photographer,
the welder, the plant manager, a cab driver, a car salesman, a
hairstylist, the gas meter reader, the supermarket box boy, the sky-
cap, housewives, executives, professional sports people, the
retired railroad engineer, the licensed practical nurse, the stone-
cutter, the librarian, the service station owner, and a host of others.

Many of those interviewed could scarcely conceal their dis-
content. "I'm a machine," says the welder. "I'm caged," says the
bank teller. "I'm a mule," says the steelworker. "I'm an object," says
the high fashion model.

Terkel begins his book by saying, "This book, being about work, is by its very nature about violence to the spirit as well as to the body. It is, above all, about daily humiliation. To survive the day is triumph enough for the walking wounded among the great many of us. It's about a search, too, for daily meaning as well as daily bread. For recognition as well as cash. For astonishment rather than torpor. In short, for a sort of life rather than a Monday-through-Friday sort of dying."[3]

One receptionist described her feelings: "Until recently, I cried in the morning. I didn't want to get up. I dreaded Fridays, because Monday was always looming over me. Another five days ahead of me. There never seemed to be any end to it. Why am I doing this? Very few people talk on the bus going home. They sort of sit there and look dejected, stare out the window, pull out the newspaper, or push other people. You feel tense until the bus empties out or you get home because the things happen to you all day long. Things you couldn't get rid of. So they build up and everybody is feeding them into each other on the bus."[4]

As I read these interviews, I wondered what could make these mundane days better. Then I read the words of a woman who works as a long-distance operator for Illinois Bell.

> Your arms don't really get tired; your mouth gets tired. It's strange, but you get tired of talking because you talk constantly for six hours without a break. It's a hard feeling when everyone's in a hurry to talk to somebody else, but not to talk to you. Sometimes you get a feeling of need to talk to somebody. It's something to run into somebody who says, "It's a nice day out, operator. How's your day been—busy? Has it been a rough day?" You're so thankful for these people, you say, "Oh yes, it's been an awful day. Thank you for asking."[5]

What small gestures can change moments, can touch time! It's the little acts that can brighten these mundane worlds. All humans desperately need a little love: a kind word spoken, a gentle tone, a smile, a thank you, appreciation, some respect, a place—be it ever so small—of significance.

The Christian who takes Christ into the workplace can find hundreds of ways to make the world a better place. The presents you give to the people you meet in the course of your daily business can be small: a personal inquiry of the telephone operator;

pleasantness while making a banking transaction; recognition for the ticket taker or the shoeshine man, the paperboy, the woman in the secretarial pool.

Often we think that if we're going to change the world, we must accomplish heroic feats. That's my bent. And it's true—acts of valor *are* needed in this world where evil leers and despair has its way.

But I think I've finally come to understand that the mighty acts are made up of multiplied thousands of small gestures. Courtesy. Giving someone a seat on a crowded commuter train. Care. Remembering to ask about the child who was sick. Mercy. Noting the date of death and making sure the widower is not lonely this first anniversary, this first Thanksgiving, this first Christmas, this first birthday alone.

The genius about God's design for Christians is that we are everywhere. I run into believers everywhere I go and they leave clues—they hum hymns under their breath! "I know that one," I said to a woman recently, a fellow hummer. "It's 'Rock of Ages, cleft for me.'" "Sure enough," she said, "I've been singing it since I was a child."

These Christians have Bibles on their desks. I made a purchase at a shop recently and noticed a chain reference Bible among the stacks of ledgers on the manager's shelf. "Whose Bible?" I inquired, and discovered it belonged to the owner of the store who took it out to study during quiet moments.

These Christians are salespeople, teachers, janitors—the list is as long as those Terkel interviewed in his book. Longer! And they, through deeds small but not unnoticed, make the world a better place. They—and you—can bring the Spirit of the living Christ to the office, to the counter, to the assembly line, to the classroom. How? Simply by caring for those around you.

A steelworker said, "You're not regarded. You're just a number out there, just like a prisoner. When you report off you tell them your badge number. A lot of people don't know your name. They know you by your badge number. My number is 440665."

But the Christian, by God's design, infiltrates the workplace and says to all men and women, "To Christ you're not a number. To Christ you are a human being of such invaluable worth that he gave his life for you so that you could live abundantly."

The beautiful thing is that we can demonstrate what Christ is like in small ways and these small acts make someone's life a little better. The many small acts total a great whole, and the workplace can be transformed.

The apostle John wrote, "You . . . are from God and have overcome them, because the one who is in you is greater than the one who is in the world" (1 John 4:4).

Let us take these words to heart. Let us think small. And let us overcome our world by many small acts of love.

K.M.

End-of-the-Day Replay

1. Remove distractions

2. Rerun the events of your day

3. Respond to Christ's evaluation

I sensed Christ said to me:

"This was well done: _____

_____

_____."

"Work harder on this: _____

_____

_____."

☐ I have established a support relationship with another Christian and am meeting at least once a week.

Imitation of Christ

Friday, Day Thirteen

Christ wants to transform my daily work. Through today's Scripture, Ephesians 4:25-32, he is saying to me specifically, "_____, *in your work situation* _____ _____."

The 1400s were years of incredible chaos. The Black Plague had just hit; on its heels came the One Hundred Years War. A fight erupted for control of the church. Bickering, feuding, corruption—it's the time when the "seven deadly sins" invaded the church in all their anger, pride, lust, envy, sloth, gluttony, and covetousness.

But during this period of darkness a glimmer of light came on the horizon. About a hundred years before Martin Luther lived a man by the name of Gerhard Grut. He wasn't a preacher, but he began to preach on the streets of a small town in Holland. He called people to turn away from sin, to be imitators of Christ, and to read God's word. Many people began to follow.

His converts began to copy Scripture to distribute within the community. Someone suggested, "Why don't you form a group?" So they did, and it came to be known as "The Brethren of the Common Life." They shared funds, pooled their resources, worked with their hands, and took care of themselves.

Simple people. *But they shone as light in the world.*

A young German boy, just twelve years old, entered that commune at his parents' request. The boy was from a small town just outside of Dusseldorf called Kempen, and eventually came to be known as Thomas a Kempis—"Thomas from Kempen."

Thomas thought that if he performed the good works modeled by this group, he would find God. But very quickly he learned that salvation comes only through Christ. Soon he submitted to his Lord. Later he became famous because of his book, a book translated more widely than any other apart from Scripture. It's called *Of the Imitation of Christ.*

I have an idea where he got that title. The apostle Paul wrote, "Be kind and compassionate to one another, forgiving each other, just as in Christ God forgave you. *Be imitators of God,* therefore, as dearly loved children and live a life of love, just as Christ loved us and gave himself up for us as a fragrant offering and sacrifice to God" (Ephesians 4:32-5:2, emphasis mine).

That's exactly what "The Brethren of the Common Life" were doing. Read a passage or two from Thomas's book:

> Endeavor to be patient in bearing with the defects and infirmities of others, of what sort soever they be, for that thyself also hast many failings which must be borne with by others.
>
> Occasions of adversity best discover how great virtue or strength each one hath.

Difficult settings are a test of how strong we are in the Lord. Dark places show our real stuff. Sometimes we don't realize the power and beauty and attractiveness of light in those settings. People notice when we're in a dark place, shining forth light. People are watching; they look at us.

We're giving the light exposure in darkness. Christians are to be bringing joy and bringing the very presence of Christ to any place we happen to be working.

Have you ever become aware of how strong your influence is or how your own light has affected people around you? In just the past couple of days, I've had two such unusual experiences.

Just the other night I got a phone call from someone whom I've met only a few times. The first time we met he had just lost his job and was very discouraged. That's a dark setting. I took time to listen, prayed with him, and later he reported back a time or two. Then just two nights ago, he called to say, "I want you to know you have been a tremendous encouragement to me. I just wanted to say, 'God bless you, I appreciate you, brother.'"

That made my day! I was overwhelmed. I didn't think what I had done was that big of a deal.

Then, yesterday, I took the time to catch up on a week's worth of mail at home. Four or five people had written to tell us how we had, in some way, touched their lives—ways that I thought were no big deal. But again I was moved. I thought, *You know, this working for Jesus stuff is OK. I like this!*

Sometimes it's not the huge things you do as much as the simple things. Someone notices, his or her life is affected, and the person is drawn to the Lord. Christ's light still shines in dark places when we imitate him.

Sometimes I think we need to be convinced about the power of light. Yes, the darkness is strong, but light can be much more powerful. Be the light of Jesus in your setting!

I recall a night many years ago in high school. It was graduation night. I had tried to live for the Lord, to walk for him. Let me tell you, that's a lonely night when you're a believer. Everyone else was going different ways. A lot of them were drinking, and I was tempted to go with them. I felt so alone.

I was walking the halls of the school one last time when a high school teacher who had meant an awful lot to me approached. I had watched him all my years of high school. He and his wife had just had a baby boy and he said to me, "Hey! I'm so glad I saw you. I wanted to tell you that my wife and I were talking, and we decided we want our son to grow up to be like you more than any other student in the high school."

I'd been watching him. I didn't realize he had been watching *me!* I hadn't been conscious of trying to do anything special. But the light of my life apparently had been shining. While it's a bit embarrassing to talk about, it's encouraging to know that the things we do on Christ's behalf are being perceived by others. And they see not primarily us, but the Lord.

So let me say to you who are in dark places: Be a light in your situation! Give away the presents of Jesus! Give away the presents of patience, of kindness. Though it may seem like an insignificant thing to you, believe me, people are watching and are being ministered to.

Notice, people are not *listening* as much as *watching*.

As I think back over Jesus' life, I think of all the individuals he touched. He brought goodness to people everywhere he went. As a result, the light of the world profoundly affected its darkness.

This day, there are people in a setting of darkness who need Christ's light. Don't miss the opportunity to share that light with them!

D.M., S.B.

End-of-the-Day Replay

1. Remove distractions

2. Rerun the events of your day

3. Respond to Christ's evaluation

I sensed Christ said to me:

"This was well done: _____

_____

_____."

"Work harder on this: _____

_____

_____."

☐ This week I gave away three presents of Christ and recorded this information on page 56.

The People's Workplace Award

Saturday, Day Fourteen

Christ wants to transform my daily work. Through today's Scripture, Psalm 122:1, he is saying to me specifically,

"_____, *in your work situation*

_____

_____ ."

I'd like to suggest a new program to replace the Academy Awards. Presenting . . . the People's Workplace Award!

This award is dedicated to those who make a difference in their daily work. I envision nominations coming from all occupational fields. While all America watches, real life workers receive recognition for their contributions to the workplace.

Wouldn't it be something when the spotlight pans to an outstanding letter carrier or woodworker? Wouldn't you like to see someone like that take a bow? Or to hear praises for a heretofore unknown, but deserving, university professor? I'd like to see our nation's most dedicated nurse come to the stage for a well-deserved round of applause. Or have Barbara Walters do an after-award interview with the leading firefighter. I'd like to cheer while the president of the United States hands out awards to people who have brought special meaning to their work, who have influenced their work world for the better.

I, for one, would like to applaud some real people who learned how to bring a sense of personal worth to their jobs—even if their tasks seem menial. These people are the real American heroes, although their sacrifices and unusual dedication more often than not go unnoticed.

I've recently become aware of many unsung heroes in all kinds of work settings. I've also become aware of some workers who deserve an award of another kind—like the guys who delivered a new mattress to our house the other day and refused to move the old bed to set up the new one, pleading "company policy." They stood around and watched while a ten-year-old neighborhood girl and I struggled with the awkward thing. Then when they saw our progress, I could almost hear them thinking, *Oh, bother! They managed to move it. Now we'll have to set up the new stuff.* They *threw* the new set together.

But I guess I can't be too hard on them. After all, as the saying goes, they were "just doing their jobs." And there are times when most of us, including myself, do the bare minimum to get that paycheck at the end of the week.

In contrast to those men, I'd like to give an award to a clerk who waited on me in a shoe store the other day. I was in a particularly indecisive mood. The boxes were piling higher when I finally made my decision. Then I noticed the shoes I selected were poorly dyed. I asked for another pair in the same size and the salesman brought out five boxes of taupe-colored 7 1/2s. That was nice of him, except that I wear a size 7. Back he went to the storeroom to get all the taupe-colored size 7s. Now the pile was huge. And I was buying only one pair!

I was embarrassed. While I thanked him for all his trouble, with discomfort I thought of how he was going to spend the next ten minutes putting away all the shoes I'd rejected. "No problem, lady, I wish all my customers were like you," he said.

"You're kidding."

"No, I don't know what it is. But it's been nice waiting on you."

Hey, if I was one of his better customers, it must really be tough being a shoe salesman these days! That man, and others like him who consistently put forth more than just the barest effort, who refuse to work on a demeaning mechanical level and instead infuse their jobs with human kindness and decency—those workers deserve to be nominated for the People's Workplace Award for Outstanding Effort on the Job. They deserve it.

But the reality is, it probably will never happen.

In the book *Working*, author Studs Terkel examines how people in various types of work struggle to find meaning in their jobs. He interviews people whose jobs don't normally give them a voice in our society.

One woman spoke of her daily dilemma: "I think most of us are looking for a calling, not just a job. Most of us, like the assembly line worker, have jobs that are too small for our spirits. Jobs are just not big enough for people."[6]

Terkel concludes, "During my three years of research for this book, I was constantly astonished by the extraordinary dreams of ordinary people. No matter how bewildering the time, those we call ordinary are aware of a sense of personal worth, or more often, a lack of it, in the work they do."

Most of us will never receive a People's Workplace Award, although I know many deserve it. Many of us will not be able to derive a sense of personal worth from the nature of our jobs alone. But in this world where few awards are given, we need to sense the joy of hearing Christ's words for outstanding achievement in the field of kindness . . . for reaching new heights in the field of loving . . . for excellent efforts in the field of bringing joy to the workplace. We long to hear him say to us, "Good job!"

When Christ spoke those reassuring words about coming to the world to give us abundant life, I'm sure he didn't intend to exclude the hours between nine and five.

If you've been giving away presents like goodness, gentleness, and peace, then you may already be experiencing a new sense of personal worth in your job. You may have sensed a new calling, discovered a renewed sense of mission, received a new lease on life in your workplace.

And here's another wonderful reality: As you become more aware of his presence in your daily work by giving away the presents of Christ, by realigning your life to the Scriptures you've read each day, by trying to close the gap between your work world and your Sunday world, you'll also be more aware of his approval of your efforts.

Are you beginning to look at your job in a whole new way? Beginning to see it through the Lord's eyes? If so, in a work world where so few find real meaning, you're receiving an award already!

May you, even today, sense the joy of Christ's words for outstanding achievement in the field of kindness . . . for reaching new heights in the field of loving . . . for excellent effort in the field of bringing joy to the workplace. May you sense him saying to you, "Good job!"

V.B.

End-of-the-Day Replay

1. Remove distractions

2. Rerun the events of your day

3. Respond to Christ's evaluation

I sensed Christ said to me:

"This was well done: _____

_____

_____."

"Work harder on this: _____

_____

_____."

☐ I remembered to pray the Ultimate Authority Prayer today.

Week Two Notes

1. Ted Rendall, *Fire in the Church* (Chicago: Moody Press, 1974) p. 19.

2. Robert E. Coleman, ed., *One Divine Moment* (Old Tappan, N.J.: Fleming H. Revell, 1970), p. 125.

3. Studs Terkel, *Working* (New York: Ballantine Books, 1985), p. xiii.

4. Ibid., pp. 59-60.

5. Ibid., pp. 67-69.

6. Ibid., pp. 716.

Treat Other Workers in a Way that Would Please Our Lord

The Bible calls us the "sweet aroma" of Christ.
Imagine how our workplaces would be affected
if we brought that fragrance with us.
Jesus' joy, patience, and love
would replace bickering and grumbling.

Week Three:
Recording Progress

Bridge the Gap between Church and Work
(Details on page 13.)

To help bridge the church/work gap I completed assignment number _____ on _____(date). The experience taught me that _____

_____

_____

_____.

Delight Others by Giving Away the Presents of Christ
(Details on page 18.)

This week I tried to delight others by giving the presents of Christ three times in the following ways:

1. On _____ I gave a present of _____

   to _____.

2. On _____ I gave a present of _____

   to _____.

3. On _____ I gave a present of _____

   to _____.

It's a Jungle Out There
Sunday, Day Fifteen

Christ wants to transform my daily work. Through today's Scripture, Galatians 6:9-10, he is saying to me specifically,
"_____, *in your work situation*

_____

_____ . "

Living for Christ on Sunday is easy compared to living for him in your daily work setting. In the church, of course, we never, EVER, have personality conflicts. People are always thanked profusely for what they do. No one suffers hurt feelings. It's been years since there have been any discernible cliques. Even the business meetings are models of peace and tranquility!

But your daily world of work—now, that's a different story. It's a jungle out there!

In grade school, kids tease you and call you names. In high school they look down on you if you wear the wrong style clothes. Homemakers have to contend with neighborhood children who rival God for being omnipresent. Employers are angry if workers arrive even a few minutes late. Employees steal anything they can get their hands on. Why, even Jesus might have a hard time trying to live by his kingdom values in some work settings.

That's why it has always confused me when I read the Gospels. It seems our Lord had his biggest problems in the synagogues among religious leaders. But in the world of fishermen, of tax collectors and soldiers and farmers, merchants, potters, teachers, artisans—there he seemed to do quite well. And to such settings he brought with him presents of love and joy and peace and kindness.

Would he be able to do it today? It's a more confusing world today, you know. We don't deal with camels, but with computer chips. It's not so much the family farm products as buying options in the futures market. And the simple shopkeeper has been all but gobbled up by franchises that compete in huge, worldwide markets.

Any one man—even if his name *is* Jesus—would have great difficulty understanding the myriad jobs in a world like ours. That's one reason I believe our Lord said it was to our advantage that he go away. With the coming of the Spirit, he could effectively take on a new body—yours and mine—and thereby become part of all the worlds where those who belong to him are involved. That is, if we allow him that opportunity.

That's part of what this spiritual adventure is all about. It's giving our Lord the privilege of living his life through us. We are the present body of Christ. He's with us on Sunday as we gather to worship him and learn of his will, and he's with us when we touch ever so many work settings on Monday and the rest of the week. If we represent him well, Christ will truly be seen in all of his beauty, even in the places where we work.

A homemaker in a high-rise apartment receives a call at an inappropriate time, asking if she would like to sign up for a lawn care service. "I'm really not interested," she responds, "but you presented your service well. I appreciate the good job you did. Have a good day as you make other calls." And Christ's joy has been released in that salesperson's pushy world.

A business associate arrives late for a meeting with his boss. He expects the worst because he knows his employer prizes punctuality. Instead he's asked, "Is everything alright? You're usually right on time. I hope nothing's wrong in the family." Through this demonstration of patience, a worker is made open to the Christ his boss serves—even though he hadn't been before.

"I don't care if you've been sick all year," says the tough high school teacher. "To get back into class you have to make up all my tests. That's just the way it is. I go by rules, not circumstances!" "And I thank you for being consistent," says the high school student who belongs to Christ. "That's a good quality." It's not an easy response. But, with Jesus' help, she gives a beautiful gift of self-control. That's important, too, because her teacher knows she's a believer.

Pah-lease, someone may be thinking, *let's be realistic, shall we? You don't know that my boss was formerly a warden at the state penitentiary! Or You weren't aware that restaurants want your business as a retiree only if you don't stay very long in a booth. Or, You don't know how tight it gets at work when deadlines are missed and how foul the tongue of my foreman gets!*

No, I don't. And I know it's not always possible to delight everyone even by giving them presents of Christ. In Scripture, certain people were even disrespectful to our Lord.

But that doesn't change the following Bible verse: "Let us not become weary in doing good, for at the proper time we will reap a harvest if we do not give up. Therefore, as we have opportunity, let us do good to all people, especially to those who belong to the family of believers" (Galatians 6:9-10).

Though Christ wasn't able to relate to all people, there were times one would have predicted failure and yet he came through in a most remarkable way. What would you say to a "woman of the night" who's been captured in the very act, brought to you, and thrown at your feet? Self-righteous men are ready to end her life. They hold good-sized stones in their hands, ready to smash her body with them. They just wait for a word from you.

I see Jesus looking in his supply of presents and choosing several for her. With few words, before long he's dispersed the crowd. One by one the accusers leave. "Has no one condemned you?" he asks. "No one, sir." "Then neither do I condemn you. Go now and leave your life of sin" (John 8:10-11).

I have a feeling that's what she did. I hope so. At least she was given a remarkable opportunity.

None of you have a work setting as painfully brutal as that of this pitiful woman-on-call. But even to the world of the prostitute, our Lord brought gentleness and kindness and patience and peace and love.

So there's no reason to think that in the difficult setting of our own work, we can't treat others in the same way. At least we can try. For his sake.

D.M.

End-of-the-Day Replay

1. Remove distractions

2. Rerun the events of your day

3. Respond to Christ's evaluation

I sensed Christ said to me:

"This was well done: _____

_____

_____."

"Work harder on this: _____

_____

_____."

☐ To bridge the church/work gap I have completed one of the weekly assignments and recorded this information on page 88.

The Best Present
I Ever Got

Monday, Day Sixteen

Christ wants to transform my daily work. Through today's

Scripture, Matthew 5:43-48, he is saying to me specifically,

"_____, *in your work situation*

_____

_____ ."

"Hey, can one of you guys get the boss a drink of water? He's thirsty!"

No big deal, right? Just a drink of water. Most office water coolers have paper cups. Anybody can do it.

Then how come a drink of water would become one of the best gifts this particular leader was ever given?

The man wanting a drink, David, would become Israel's second king. At the time, he was in a cave hiding out from his enemies. A garrison of Philistines was stationed in Bethlehem and David longed for a cool drink of water from the well in his hometown.

It had to have been a casual remark. David didn't expect anyone to take him seriously. I'm sure he was thirsty, but to require a drink from this particular well wasn't necessary.

93

Three special friends of David, however, heard his comment. These three—Josheb, Eleazar, and Shammah, "the three mighty men"—admired and loved their leader. Together they said, "Let's get him what he wants."

"So the three mighty men broke through the Philistine lines, drew water from the well near the gate of Bethlehem and carried it back to David" (2 Samuel 23:16).

Wow! Try telling someone in the lunchroom to get you a drink of water because you're thirsty. How do you think they'd respond? If you're choking to death on the cafeteria beef stew, someone might smack you on the back a time or two. But get a drink for you? Forget it!

Well, here were three choice men who risked their very lives to get David what he casually mentioned at a time of pressure. How's that for an act of loyalty? Of love? Of kindness?

David was deeply touched. He wouldn't even drink the water, protesting that it would be like drinking the blood of those who risked their lives for him. Scripture again: "Far be it from me, O LORD, to do this." And he poured it out as an offering to God. The water had become sacred to him.

Do you think David quickly forgot what these three friends did for him? Do you suppose that after some years he might have said, "What's a glass of water, anyway?"

Not on your life!

I've discovered that many times people remember with fondness the small things I do more than the expensive ones. A specific something met a need—much like David's irrational need for a drink from the well at Bethlehem.

My daily work before coming to the "Chapel of the Air" was as pastor in the inner city of Chicago. During my family's twelve years there we carried on extensive ministry among the poor. A good lesson I learned was that I didn't have to figure out how to minister to these good people. I was much better off if I didn't think about it too much.

What I needed was to listen to them talk. They could tell me where they were hurting. It would have been presumptuous to say, "Let me explain what you need." I wasn't on welfare. I'd never had my heat shut off or gone hungry. I had a job with a steady salary.

So when these parents, mostly mothers, said what they wanted, the requests weren't that hard to meet:

- Someone to help a child with his studies.
- A drive in the country with woods like those remembered from childhood days.
- A Bible of her own.
- Prayer.

The truth is, these dear folk often gave me presents that cost more than the ones I gave them. Like a special meal of fried chicken and all that goes with it. Or a birthday present for little Randy so he would have something to play with "while you're spending so much time helping us folk." Or a chocolate cake with frosting just the way I like it.

Bless them all! Yet they saw *me* as the giver. In their minds, I was the one doing all the reaching out. Maybe it was just that nobody else said to them, "Tell me where you hurt, and I'll see what I or the church can do for you."

Are there folks in need at your daily work? Maybe it's the man or woman who recently lost a member of the family. What would such a person want? Something expensive? I doubt it. But I'd bet he or she would very much appreciate a chance to talk about that special loved one who's now missing.

Maybe it's someone you normally think of as strong, but pressures have caused that invincibility to melt. What are his words or actions saying? "Someone please help"? And how? By offering to pay for professional counseling? No. "Just ask me about the pressures I'm facing. Or pray with me."

Or the person who's suddenly angry with everyone. Why? Because she just got mean all of a sudden? "I want to know what's really bothering you," you say. Then you hear how her parents are getting a divorce. "I'm so sorry," you tell her, "is there anything I can do?" "No, nothing." But when you leave, she says, "Thanks."

Why "thanks"? Because you listened. To her, it was a present of kindness. Sometimes it's a matter of not thinking so much about your words or deeds as it is of listening, really listening, to others.

"Ah, that I could have a drink of water from the well near the Bethlehem gate!" I imagine a lot of people heard David's remark.

But three men really heard it. And they ministered to the one who would one day be king.

If you listen closely to people at work, you too can minister effectively on Christ's behalf. Remember your king's words in Matthew 10:42: "If anyone gives a cup of cold water to one of these little ones, . . . he will certainly not lose his reward."

One last word of advice: Relax regarding this assignment. Stop trying to figure out what you'll do for someone, and just listen. Really listen. And take your cues from that.

D.M.

End-of-the-Day Replay

1. Remove distractions

2. Rerun the events of your day

3. Respond to Christ's evaluation

I sensed Christ said to me:

"This was well done: _____

_____

_____."

"Work harder on this: _____

_____

_____."

☐ I am remembering this week to give away three of the presents of Christ and to record this information on page 88.

Live Again through Me

Tuesday, Day Seventeen

Christ wants to transform my daily work. Through today's Scripture, 1 Timothy 2:1-4, he is saying to me specifically,

"_____, *in your work situation*

_____

_____."

If Christ walked this land today and ministered as he once did in Palestine, I'm convinced he would frequently show up at a factory, a school, a government office building, a television studio—any place of work. He wouldn't be seen or heard exclusively at churches or Bible conferences.

Don't get me wrong. People work in those settings as well, and pastors put in long hours, as do directors of camps and conference grounds. My point is that Christ was not unfamiliar with what most people see as the workplace.

As you read through the Gospels, the list of jobs touched by Christ in one way or another is quite remarkable. Fishermen, soldiers, political figures, tax collectors, farmers, homemakers, servants, jailers, shepherds, musicians, doctors, the poor who grub for a living, beggars, prostitutes, lawyers, potters, mourners, jewelers, writers, roofers, shopkeepers, moneylenders, tanners, builders, athletes, students, teachers, cooks, clothiers, judges, carpenters, vine-growers, stonemasons, investors, banquet caterers, metal workers, tent makers . . . the list goes on and on.

If he were here today, Christ wouldn't move solely in the subculture of the church. He'd be out in the world, touching lives, helping the hurting.

He's not here today . . . but he is. Today, all believers make up the body of Christ in the world. As once Jesus walked in the flesh and people could see and hear and touch him, so they still can. The body of Christ can be seen and heard and touched as our Lord lives his life through us.

Talk about infiltrating the workplace!

If you thought the earlier list of jobs was long, I could take from now until next Tuesday just to name different places of work where Christ will be present this very day, through his Spirit. He truly lives in all his people!

The question is whether these believers will allow the Lord to live out his life through them. If they will, he will transform their daily work as surely as Christ would were he present in the flesh.

Dr. Walter Wilson was a physician and an excellent teacher of God's word. Later he became a pastor of a large church, and today his name is connected with Kansas City Bible College.

On January 14, 1914, Dr. Wilson went to hear Dr. James M. Gray preach on Romans 12:1. Gray was a clergyman of the Reformed Episcopal Church and later would be president of the Moody Bible Institute. "Leaning over the pulpit," writes Wilson, "he said, 'Have you noticed that this verse does not tell us to whom we should give our bodies? It is not the Lord Jesus who asks for it. He has His own body. It is not the Father who asks for it. He remains upon His throne. Another has come to earth without a body. God could have made a body for Him as he did for Jesus, but he did not do so. God gives you the privilege and the indescribable honor of presenting your bodies to the Holy Spirit, to be His dwelling place here on earth. . . Will you do so now?' "

In the book *They Found the Secret*, Dr. V. Raymond Edman, president of Wheaton College, tells what happened next.

> At the conclusion of the service Dr. Wilson. . . returned home. Utterly heartbroken over his fruitless life, yet filled with a great hope because of the message. . . Dr. Wilson lay upon the carpet of his study, prostrate in God's presence. Hear his testimony:

"There, in the quiet of that late hour, I said to the Holy Spirit, 'My Lord, I have mistreated you all my Christian life. . . When I wanted You I called for You: I have sought to use You only as a willing servant to help me in my self-appointed and chosen work. I shall do so no more. Just now I give you this body of mine; from my head to my feet, I give it to You. I give You my hands, my limbs, my eyes and my lips, my brain; all that I am within and without, I hand over to You for You to live in it the life that You please. You may send this body to Africa, or lay it on a bed with cancer. You may blind the eyes, or send me with Your message to Tibet. . . It is Your body from this moment on. Help Yourself to it. Thank you, my Lord. I believe you have accepted it, for in Romans 12 and 1, you said "acceptable to God. . . " We now belong to each other.' "

The very next morning two young ladies came to the office to sell advertising, as they had done previously. Up to that time the doctor had never spoken to them about the Lord Jesus because his lips had been his own. . . Now that his lips had been given away, the Holy Spirit was to use them. . . Out of a brief conversation and testimony to his visitors, Dr. Wilson led both of them to a saving knowledge of Jesus Christ. They were the first fruits of a great harvest of souls that Dr. Wilson has won for the Savior.[1]

One day Wilson traveled alone to New York City. "Before he went out for a business appointment he had prayed in his hotel room, and requested, "My Lord, this is a large city. . . and I am just a weak, unknown servant of Thine with. . . no acquaintance with the hungry hearts that may be there. Thou alone dost know whom thou has been dealing with. Here is my body—my feet and my lips. Wilt Thou take them today to some troubled heart and speak through me Thy words of light and life?"

As he walked eastward on Thirty-second Street, Wilson passed a stationery shop and noticed a small, leather-covered notebook in the window. When he purchased it he asked the little German owner, "Do you know what I expect to do with this little book?" The shopkeeper didn't know, and was astonished to learn that it was to be used as a prayer book.

"I am sorry, my friend, but this is a blank book," he said. "It is not a prayer book."

That was the opening Dr. Wilson needed. He explained how he wrote down his prayer requests and gave his testimony of knowing

Christ. "I have tried to find Gott for many years," came the reply. "I have gone around Manhattan and Brooklyn and the Bronx, night after night, attending many services, but failed always to find Gott. Can you tell me how to get to him?" Dr. Wilson could and did. Not more than twenty minutes had elapsed from his prayer in the hotel room until this shopkeeper was kneeling at the cross.

It's thrilling, isn't it? If all believers gave the Holy Spirit permission to use their bodies as he wanted, do you think our work worlds would be impacted?

Let me ask Dr. James M. Gray's question of you today, just the way he asked it the night Dr. Walter Wilson was listening on January 14, 1914.

"God gives you the privilege and the indescribable honor of presenting your bodies to the Holy Spirit. And will you do so?"

D.M.

End-of-the-Day Replay

1. Remove distractions

2. Rerun the events of your day

3. Respond to Christ's evaluation

I sensed Christ said to me:

"This was well done: _____

_____

_____."

"Work harder on this: _____

_____

_____."

☐ I remembered to pray the Ultimate Authority Prayer today.

Be a Perk Provider
Wednesday, Day Eighteen

Christ wants to transform my daily work. Through today's

Scripture, Hebrews 13:5-6, he is saying to me specifically,

"_____, in your work situation

_____

_____."

In the context of work, what do the following three events have in common?

- A farewell luncheon
- A retirement dinner
- A funeral

If you're thinking a meal is served at all three occasions, that's not what I have in mind. A more obvious similarity: Each occasion is designed to give special attention to just one individual. Typically, speeches are given honoring the person or employee who is leaving or retiring or who is deceased.

Most employed people attend occasions such as these at least once or so a year. Have you ever thought, like I have, *It's a shame it takes a token event like this to motivate people to make such kind and wonderful statements*?

Wouldn't it be better if this positive input were provided along the way instead of waiting until a person leaves or retires or dies? Dying is pretty serious!

I've worked at a few places over the past twenty years where leaving has been made to look pretty attractive. At one place in particular, so much effort went into giving proper farewells—parties, luncheons, cards, gifts, speeches highlighting the person's abilities and special accomplishments—that whenever an employee left, I always had to wonder, *If these kinds of things had been done or said a lot earlier, maybe he or she would have stuck around.*

These flashy send-offs were sometimes counterproductive to those of us who stayed behind. More than once I thought, *If you have to leave to get perks, then maybe I should move on, too.*

Let's face it. All of us have a need to be noticed. We like it when someone says, "Nice job. You're a hard worker. You add a lot to this place. You're really skilled at what you do."

Just last week I heard about a church in Minnesota that gave its pastor and his wife a surprise reception following a Sunday service for no other reason than to say, "We appreciate you. Thanks for who you are and for all your good work." You can bet that couple will be there for awhile!

I'm thoroughly convinced that most people in today's work force don't receive the credit due them. For the majority, perks are few and far between. I'd guess that only a small percentage receives any kind of input about job performance.

Regardless of how you spend your working hours—studying, cutting deals, solving technical problems, taking care of children, fixing cars, cleaning, looking after the elderly or the ill, typing, delivering the mail, teaching—everyone, including you and me, needs occasional perks to stay fresh.

But, as needful as that is, I believe we should be more concerned about something else: To what extent do you and I give away perks? And how accomplished are we at providing positive input for others?

What if Jesus had your job? How do you suppose he would relate to the people in your workplace? How would he act? Would his presence be felt? Do you think his being there would make a difference?

You know it would! He'd bring a breath of fresh air to your place of work.

I'm sure his first priority would be to learn everyone's name. Then he'd begin to ask questions showing personal interest in each individual. It wouldn't take him long to say something posi-tive about everybody—even that "difficult" person. He'd be espe-cially sensitive to those who were struggling. And he'd still be cooperative and cheerful if the boss happened to change plans and redistribute tasks.

Jesus doing your job would make a refreshing difference in your workplace. In fact, *you* doing your job with the awareness of Jesus' presence could make a considerable impact!

An incident in the Old Testament shows what I mean. In Exodus 18, Moses received word that his father-in-law, Jethro, was coming to visit him in the desert. Jethro was anxious to hear first-hand how Moses was handling his work, which was leading the people of Israel out of Egypt.

When Jethro arrived, Moses told him everything the Lord had done to the Egyptians, all about Israel's hardships along the way, and how the Lord had saved them. The text says, "Jethro was delighted to hear about all" these good things. An excellent illus-tration of personal interest in someone's daily work!

The next day on the job, when Moses took his seat as judge, needy people stood all around from morning until evening. When his father-in-law saw all that Moses was doing, he gave some valu-able input.

"Moses," he said, "you're going to wear yourself out. The work's too heavy for you. You can't handle it all alone. I have a bet-ter idea—see if you like it."

After he explained his plan to delegate some of the responsi-bility to make the work load lighter, Jethro said to Moses, "If you do this, and if God so commands, you'll be able to stand the strain and all the people will go home satisfied."

Scripture tells us that Moses listened and did everything his father-in-law suggested. The new organizational chart was imple-mented and proved most successful. Not only did Jethro's brief but positive input add to the effectiveness of Moses' daily work, but an entire nation benefited for years to come.

Wouldn't it have been tragic had Jethro said nothing? What if he had kept himself busy just minding his own affairs? Or what if he had been disinterested? Who knows? Without Jethro's help, Moses might have grown dissatisfied with his performance on the job. Maybe he would have looked for another line of work or decided to take an early retirement. Perhaps the mounting stress would have taken its toll and put Moses into an early grave.

I'm sure lots of nice things would have been said at his farewell luncheon, or his retirement dinner, or his funeral—but thank the Lord Jethro said something earlier instead of later!

So what am I driving at? Just this: I'm encouraging you to continue giving away the presents of Christ—the present of patience, the present of goodness, the present of joy, and all the others.

Generously giving away the presents of Christ provides needed refreshment, especially in the workplace. So be a perk provider. Be a generous dispenser of Christ's presence. And discover how much of Jethro lives in *you*.

S.B.

End-of-the-Day Replay

1. Remove distractions

2. Rerun the events of your day

3. Respond to Christ's evaluation

I sensed Christ said to me:

"This was well done: _____

_____

_____."

"Work harder on this: _____

_____

_____."

☐ I have given away at least one of the presents of Christ this week and have recorded this information on page 88.

Fear of Man
Thursday, Day Nineteen

Christ wants to transform my daily work. Through today's Scripture, Proverbs 29:25, he is saying to me specifically,
"_____, *in your work situation*
_____
_____ ."

DAVID: Why don't more Christians influence their work setting for Christ? One of the main reasons is found in Proverbs 29:25: "Fear of man will prove to be a snare; but whoever trusts in the LORD is kept safe." Has that ever been a problem for you, Karen?

KAREN: In high school I was worried about peer pressure. But our Christian youth leaders challenged us to carry our Bibles every day. Mine was big and red. I carried it for two years on top of my books, and I think that pretty much put to death the fear of man in me.

DAVID: During high school I also had to decide whether I was going to take a stand. And I thought the problem was licked. But it's one of those that rears its head every so often. Am I going to speak out for Jesus, or am I going to back off?

KAREN: It's a major problem in the workplace. People are worried about being fired. They're worried about the opinion of their co-workers. They're worried about not getting a job advancement. It becomes a bondage, an emotional, spiritual, psychological bondage.

DAVID: That was the problem with William P. Nicholson, a great Christian man who was converted during the English revivals of the early 1900s. According to V. Raymond Edman in his book, *They Found the Secret*, Nicholson wrote:

> The fear of man was a dreadful snare and I was helplessly caught by it. I was ashamed of Christ and ashamed of being seen with out-and-out Christians! I was a sneak and a coward, if ever there was one. I despised myself, but was helpless about it. . .

> The Salvation Army had come to our town. The Corps was composed of two wee girls in uniform. They held open-air meetings and made a noise with their tambourines. Their first soldier was a man called Daft Jimmy. He had hardly enough brains to give him a headache, but he had sense enough to get saved. He carried the flag as they marched the streets. On his jersey, a red one, he had the women put with white yarn these words on his back, "Saved from public opinion."

> I was told by Satan that I would have to go to the open-air meeting and march down the street with two wee girls and a fool. . . I would be laughed at by all my friends. I would lose my reputation.

> I said, "Lord, I will be willing to go to Timbuctoo or Hong Kong, or even die decently as a martyr"—I couldn't get out of it. I became more and more miserable and, oh, so hungry for freedom and victory.

> At last I became desperate. I made the complete, unconditional surrender. I cried out, "Come in. Come in, Holy Spirit. Thy work of great blessing begin."

> Hallelujah! What a thrill, what a peace, what a joy!. . . As I walked down the street that Saturday it seemed as if every friend and relative I ever had were out and about. When I came to the open-air meeting and saw the two wee Salvation Army girls singing and rattling their tambourines, and poor Daft Jimmy holding the flag, I nearly turned back. Talk about dying! I was dying hard that night. I stepped off the footpath and stood in the ring. The soldier looked at me. Then to my horror one of them said, "The people don't stop and listen: let us get down on our knees and pray." What could I do? I couldn't run away. So down I got on my knees.

The crowd gathered around. I could hear their laughter and jeers. The officer prayed a telegram prayer—short and to the point. I could have wished the prayer had been as long as the 119th Psalm. I stood up, blushing and nervous. They got the collection while the crowd was there and then to my horror, she said, "Brother! Take this tambourine and lead the march down the street to the Barracks." I couldn't let a girl beat me, so I took it. That did it. My shackles fell off, and I was free; my fears all gone.

I started down the street, whether in the body or out of the body, I can't tell. I lost my reputation, and fear of man: joy and peace and glory filled me. . . I lost something that night I never want to find again, and I found something I never want to lose. That is, I lost my reputation and fear of man, and found the joy and peace of the overflowing fullness of the Spirit. Hallelujah![2]

Edman tells another story that took place April 21, 1855. Edward Kimball, a Sunday school teacher, had decided that day he would speak to a young man about Christ. He wrote,

I started down to Holton's shoe store. When I was nearly there I began to wonder whether I ought to go just then during business hours. And I thought maybe my mission might embarrass the boy, that when I went away the other clerks might ask who I was, and when they learned might taunt [him] and ask if I was trying to make a good boy out of him. While I was pondering over it all I passed the store without noticing it. Then, when I found I had gone by the door I determined to make a dash for it and have it over at once.

Kimball found who he was looking for in the back part wrapping up shoes in paper and stacking them on shelves. "I went up to him, put my hand on his shoulder, and as I leaned over I placed my foot upon a shoe box." And looking down into his eyes, Kimball made what he thought afterward was a very weak plea. He never could recall the exact words, but he asked him to come to Christ, who loved him and wanted his love and should have it, and there were tears in his eyes. It seemed that the young man was just ready for the light that broke upon him, for there, at once, in the back of the shoe store in Boston, D. L. Moody gave himself and his life to Christ.[3]

Isn't that marvelous? Choosing to make Christ your ultimate authority will free you from the bondage of the fear of man. It's not

always easy! Although we know in our minds that it's more important to please Christ than to please people, sometimes it's much
easier to see people than to see Christ.

That's why praying the Ultimate Authority Prayer is so helpful.
It reminds us how important it is that Jesus approve of what we
do. As we pray it day after day, we'll begin to sense the strong presence of Christ in our own work settings. And the fear of man will, at
last, fall away.

D.M., K.M.

End-of-the-Day Replay

1. Remove distractions

2. Rerun the events of your day

3. Respond to Christ's evaluation

I sensed Christ said to me:

"This was well done: _____

_____

_____."

"Work harder on this: _____

_____

_____."

☐ I have established a support relationship with another
Christian and am meeting at least once a week.

Any Fish, Girl?

Friday, Day Twenty

Christ wants to transform my daily work. Through today's Scripture, John 17:14-19, he is saying to me specifically,
"_____, *in your work situation*

_____

_____."

Most people have mixed feelings about their daily work. They enjoy some things but are frustrated by others.

A farmer loves working out-of-doors but must cope with the capriciousness of the weather. A teacher loves the learning process but must deal with classroom discipline. Even if you love everything about your daily work, you probably can still identify with that poor little donut maker who, facing his daily task yet again, groans those exhaustion-laden words, "Time to make the donuts."

I don't know what specific "donuts" you face in your daily work, but I do know you have them. So do I. Even while I worked through the concepts for today about Christ as the ultimate authority in the workplace, I began to wonder how well I recognized Christ as the ultimate authority in my work.

I've begun to suspect lately that there's been a conflicting voice sounding in my life. My job as program director at the "Chapel of the Air" makes me feel like that little man who, every day, has to make the donuts—and I've fallen behind in making mine.

Deadlines have come and gone and may pass by again, for there are new complications at my house. Steve, my formerly healthy husband, has broken his ankle. My last three days have been an odyssey to his bed on various missions of mercy. (*Maestro,* the violins, please.) I've been climbing so many stairs I feel like I'm in training for the Olympics. On my many trips up and down I must pass a plasterer who is fixing damage from a burst water pipe in our stairwells. Tiptoeing over his drop cloths, picking my way through broken plaster and tools, watching my house become covered with fine grit from the sanding—I feel my life passing out of my control. Today the living room ceiling is being repaired. It's like someone has draped my entire life in drop cloths and I can't get anything done.

In the midst of this frustrating and unproductive week, I found myself thinking, *How am I ever going to catch up? In all this confusion, I can't even think straight!*

Sound like your world? Well, does Scripture have much to say about modern job stresses? Are there any clues about handling our work-related tensions?

I think so. One especially interesting passage from John 21 deals with productivity in the workplace.

The disciples' lives had been in tumult those past few weeks. They'd felt helpless as they'd watched their Lord's murder. They'd been amazed, even incredulous, at his resurrection. And yet, even in the midst of their personal turmoil and wonder, their lives had to go on. Their families still had to be fed. Taxes had to be paid.

The donuts still had to be made.

One night they went fishing. They worked all night and caught nothing (*maestro,* an encore, please). Not one fish. Zero. John didn't record their words, but we can imagine their frustration when the tried-and-true tricks of the trade failed to net any result. Perhaps they salted the water with pieces of bait to attract larger fish. Maybe they dragged their nets slowly across the bottom of the lake, trying to find just the right spot. Probably they strained their eyes in the dark to discover if other boats had better luck. They must have wondered at their lack of success. *Why aren't we catching anything? We've been here all night! What a waste! We'll never catch anything at this rate. We'll probably starve!*

And then they heard another voice. "Any fish, boys?" One word records their sulky reply: "No." Then this advice: "Throw out your net on the right-hand side of the boat and you'll get plenty of them."

So they did. And not only did they catch plenty of fish, John says they couldn't pull in the net because of the weight of the fish! There they were, grunting and heaving and bending over the side of the boat and laughing at each other and at the flip-flopping catch beneath them. Then it suddenly hit: "It's the Lord!"

It's the Lord. Who else would know about good fishing places? Who else could turn an unproductive workday into a successful one? Who's a better authority on our daily work?

One definition of authority is "an individual appealed to as an expert." Christ's authority isn't confined to knowledge about fishing techniques of the first century. He knows about your work and he knows about mine. He's the ultimate consultant, the most dependable mentor. He's a specialist in your line of work. In fact, he's better at your work than you'll ever be—even if you're the best around.

How foolish we are when we try to accomplish our daily tasks without consulting him! We must learn to quiet the inner voice that tells us to try to solve our work problems by ourselves, and instead learn to ask for help from our ultimate authority, Christ.

When the stress of our daily work loads and our lack of success are as obvious as the disciples' empty nets, we need to look to the Lord. In fact, it's a good idea to ask for help even before our nets hit the water. You can pray, as I'm learning to, "Lord, help me be creative this week. Not in my own thoughts, but yours." Or when I can't get it all done: "Help me to prioritize my day. Help me to use my time productively."

And he will!

I like his words in Psalm 32:8: "I will instruct you and teach you in the way you should go; I will guide you with My eye" (NKJV).

I'm learning to recognize that voice when it asks, "Any fish, girl?" Maybe the Lord has been trying to get your attention lately through obvious questions about your daily work. Why not ask him to help you? I know he wants to. And I pray you'll recognize his voice when he calls.

When you do this, expect your nets to grow full, groaning with great ideas and solutions to your own occupational challenges. May you, today, laugh with awe at the abundance of his great help.

V.B.

End-of-the-Day Replay

1. Remove distractions
2. Rerun the events of your day
3. Respond to Christ's evaluation

I sensed Christ said to me:

"This was well done: _____

_____

_____."

"Work harder on this: _____

_____

_____."

☐ This week I gave away three presents of Christ and recorded this information on page 88.

God's Labor Contract
Saturday, Day Twenty-One

Christ wants to transform my daily work. Through today's Scripture, Isaiah 58:13-14, he is saying to me specifically,
"_____, *in your work situation*

_____

_____ ."

Ever since man has been forced to work for someone else, there's been a lament about the boss, about the job chief, about the foreman, about the commander, about the mistress, about the feudal landowner. You can see this graphically in the labor songs of the mid- to late 1800s. The working men and women of America were singing tongue-in-cheek complaints about the nature of work and specifically about the bosses, the foremen who extracted a day's labor for a pittance of pay.

One of those songs was published in 1888, "Drill Ye Terriers, Drill." The author was Thomas Casey, who, like the laborers in his song, blasted and drilled in rock quarries. It goes like this:

Every morning at seven o'clock
there were twenty terriers a drillin' on the rock,
and the boss comes along and he says, "Keep still,
and come down heavy on that cast iron drill!"

Our new foreman was Gene McCann,
and he was a blaming man.
Last week a premature blast went off
and a mile in the air went Big Jim Goff.

Next time payday came around,
Jim Goff a dollar short was found.
When asked what for, came this reply,
"You're docked for the time you was up in the sky,"

And drill ye terriers, drill!
And drill ye terriers, drill!
For it's work all day
for the sugar in your tea,
down behind the railway.
And drill ye terriers, drill!

Because the early factory and mine owners often ignored the welfare of their employees, the workers of the 1800s organized unions and sought to better their wages and working conditions. Organizers worked for an eight-hour workday, for the abolition of child labor, for more safety on the job, and for other reforms. This, too, is captured in the music of America. The song "Eight Hours" appeared after the Civil War, when organized labor began a serious campaign for an eight-hour workday. It became the official song of the movement and was sung at the first May Day celebration in the United States in 1886. Note these words:

We mean to make things over,
we are tired of toil for naught,
with but bare enough to live upon,
and nere an hour for thought.
We want to feel the sunshine
and we want to smell the flowers.
We are sure that God has willed it,
and we mean to have eight hours!
We're summoning our forces
from the shipyard, shop and mill,

   Eight hours for work,
   eight hours for rest,
   eight hours for what we will.

Hurrah! Hurrah! for labor,
for it shall arise in might.
It has filled the world with plenty,

114

it shall fill the world with light
Hurrah! Hurrah! for labor
it is mustering all its powers,
and shall march along to victory
with a banner of the hours;
shall shout the echoing rally
'til all the world can thrill!

> Eight hours for work,
> eight hours for rest,
> eight hours for what we will!

When I read about the history of the labor movement with its inherent conflict between management and workers; when I hear of gripes about the workplace, about the dehumanizing trend of our technological revolution; when I listen to these old work songs that complain about bosses, I'm reminded that I, a Christian, have an ultimate authority. Ultimately, my boss is God. And my heart lifts, and suddenly I am glad.

Jesus is a boss who has my best welfare at heart. He not only provides me with daily work, he's devised a benefit plan that lasts for eternity. I'm allowed to own shares in his kingdom project, with dividends that pay now and after death. He's not only hired me, he bought me for himself at great price.

This boss not only practices the recommended new management theory—"management by walking around" (meaning the boss is available on the floor)—my boss comes with me to my workplace. He sticks with me and helps me to do my best.

But the greatest sign of his care is his contract with me. At the beginning he established a work/rest plan intended to free me from the grind of making a living. I'll never have to boycott this boss to achieve my eight hours. I'll never have to negotiate another contract with him. Nor will I have to orchestrate a slowdown with my co-workers to demonstrate the seriousness of our demands. Nor will I ever have to strike to settle a labor/management dispute.

My heavenly boss, who's my ultimate authority, has already provided not eight hours, not sixteen, but twenty-four hours for rest from work. And this he gives me, week after week, fifty-two weeks a year—or what equals almost seven-and-one-half full weeks of vacation per year. What's more, these terms are irrevocable, written forever into a divine contract between himself and man. "Six days you shall labor, but the seventh day is a Sabbath to the LORD your God."

Let us, who are Christians, always remember that God is our ultimate authority. Let us nurture grateful hearts for the labor contract our true Boss has negotiated between himself and mankind.

He has given us rest from our labors. And because of this, let us be glad.

K.M.

End-of-the-Day Replay

1. Remove distractions

2. Rerun the events of your day

3. Respond to Christ's evaluation

I sensed Christ said to me:

"This was well done: _____

_____

_____."

"Work harder on this: _____

_____

_____."

☐ I remembered to pray the Ultimate Authority Prayer today.

Week Three Notes ────────────────────────

1. Dr. V. Raymond Edman, *They Found the Secret* (Grand Rapids: Zondervan, 1960) pp. 107-110.

2. Ibid., pp. 107-110.

3. Ibid., pp. 107-110.

Make Wise Decisions When Experiencing Two-world Tensions

It isn't easy being the subject of the King and working in a world that doesn't know him. Jesus gives us the strength we need to be "in the world, but not of it."

Week Four:
Recording Progress

Bridge the Gap between Church and Work
(Details on page 13.)

To help bridge the church/work gap I completed assignment num-

ber _____ on _____(date). The experience taught

me that _____

_____

_____

_____.

---

*Delight Others by Giving Away
the Presents of Christ*
(Details on page 18.)

This week I tried to delight others by giving the presents of Christ
three times in the following ways:

1. On _____ I gave a present of _____

   to _____.

2. On _____ I gave a present of _____

   to _____.

3. On _____ I gave a present of _____

   to _____.

It's a Part of the Territory
Sunday, Day Twenty-Two

Christ wants to transform my daily work. Through today's
Scripture, Colossians 3:22-4:1, he is saying to me specifically,
"_____, *in your work situation*

_____

_____. "

Tension.

Whether your daily work involves being a high-level executive or just being a kid in the sixth grade, third seat, second row from the windows, tension is part of the territory.

Are you sometimes tempted to cheat just to make things more even? Do you hear profanity so much that you find yourself repeating the same words in your head—or with your mouth? What do you do when somebody tells an off-color joke or shows a dirty picture?

Tension.

Homemakers feel pressure to take jobs outside the home in order to help the family income. Opposite pressures are applied from those who insist a mother's first obligation is to the family. And then there's schooling choices for the kids—public school, private school, or home schooling?

Tension!

In the factory you have been trying to show Christ's love to someone who works in the same department. Sensing you care, this individual asks a favor: Will you punch out his time card as you leave? He wants to skip out a little early. And suddenly you have a dilemma you hadn't asked for.

Tension!

Even people who are incredibly successful in their daily work face tension. A man who built two broken-down stores into the nation's largest drugstore chain said, "A typical HEADACHE of operating a public company like mine is keeping stockholders happy." Most of you don't face that problem, do you?

Maybe I'm giving you a headache just bringing up such matters! You know only too well these pressures. So what about it—is there a miracle cure? A pill that will make the unscrupulous boss just vanish—POOF!

Well, there's no pill but there is a cure. Just being a Christian resolves certain problems—not all of them, but some of them. That's what Jack Eckerd of Eckerd Drugstores found out. "When he gave Christ control of his life, Jack Eckerd changed," wrote Charles Colson in the afterword to Eckerd's book, *Eckerd: Finding the Right Prescription.* "Friends who had known him for many years now describe him as more at peace with himself, less impatient with others, better able to love and to be loved. His employees could see it! His secretary of many years remarked that he is a totally different person."

But Eckerd's new faith in Christ also brought him *new* tensions. A few days after his conversion, he walked into one of his drugstores, looked at the magazine racks, and saw what he had seen thousands of times. But this time he saw it through new eyes and was horrified to find *Playboy* and *Penthouse* on sale in his "family" stores.

"No problem," you say. "Toss them out!" But when you own seventeen hundred drugstores across America, you're talking about millions and millions of dollars . . . and what about those stockholders?

Tension. It's hard to escape even when you walk with Christ.

So what do you do when faced with such tensions? I'll tell you: When facing the two-boss tension, claim the promise of

Christ's presence. And don't wait until you're trapped in the pressure cooker to do it! Rather, in the course of the everyday, again and again remind yourself of the wonder of his presence.

That's what Jack Eckerd did. He threw out the magazines, saying, "Why else would I throw a few million dollars out the window? The reason was simple: The Lord wouldn't let me off the hook."

It was Christ's presence that brought about the change in this man's life. He had no miracle pill that would make his bosses vanish. But there was something he could do to make his heavenly boss *appear.*

Let's allow Chuck Colson to finish the story for us:

> Jack Eckerd wrote to the presidents of other drug chains describing what he had done, testifying that removing these pornographic materials hadn't killed him business-wise, and he nudged them in the same direction. No one answered his letters. After all, pornography is a profitable business! But encouraged by Eckerd's asking, thousands of Christians, organized under the National Coalition Against Pornography, were taking their stand as well—through widespread picketing and a boycott of stores selling "adult magazines."

> The pressure began to pay off. Like dominoes, stores began to remove *Playboy* and *Penthouse*; one by one, Revco, People's, Rite Aid, Dart Drug, Gray Drug, and High's Dairy Stores all pulled pornography from their shelves. Finally, the last major holdout gave in as well: 7-11 removed pornography from its forty-five hundred stores and recommended that its thirty-six hundred franchises do the same. . . .

> What couldn't be accomplished by passing laws or fighting in courts was accomplished when a man gave his life to Christ and surrendered to his lordship. The pornography industry is on the run; in the last year smut has been eliminated from fifteen thousand retail outlets—and it all started with Jack Eckerd's conversion. Don't tell me one man can't make a difference!

> This is the way God has always worked—not through institutions and governments, but through individuals he has chosen . . . that's what the gospel is all about for Jack Eckerd, and for every one of us.[1]

123

How about you? Is that what the gospel is all about to you? By following Christ's call, you can make a difference right where you are, right in your own workplace. And you don't have to be a Jack Eckerd. All you have to be is obedient.

D.M.

End-of-the-Day Replay

1. Remove distractions

2. Rerun the events of your day

3. Respond to Christ's evaluation

I sensed Christ said to me:

"This was well done: _____

_____

_____."

"Work harder on this: _____

_____

_____."

☐ To bridge the church/work gap I have completed one of the weekly assignments and recorded this information on page 120.

Intimidation

Monday, Day Twenty-Three

Christ wants to transform my daily work. Through today's Scripture, Matthew 22:15-22, he is saying to me specifically,
" _____, in your work situation

_____

_____ . "

———
———
███

Three believers, longtime friends, worked for the government. Together they held positions that were quite high. The man to whom they answered had a temper that was legendary; no one wanted to get on his bad side. Nevertheless these three managed to do it, and the conflict related to their faith.

Have you ever been in such a setting? Maybe the boss asked you to do something unethical, to say he finished a task before he really did. Or to report he wasn't in when he was.

Possibly your daily work is that of a homemaker. Your non-Christian neighbor would really profit from the neighborhood Bible study of which you're a part, but for some reason you're tongue-tied whenever you start to extend an invitation her way.

Intimidation. The word comes from the Latin *timidus*, or "afraid," which also gives us our word *timid*. Being intimidated is to be frightened, fearful, scared, alarmed by what might happen.

Whatever the situation that turns your spiritual legs to jelly, I guarantee it wasn't as bad as that facing the three men I mentioned earlier.

Their boss had made a huge image of himself, ninety feet high and nine feet wide. Governors, judges, advisors, treasurers, magistrates, and all the provincial officers assembled for the dedication of the image this man had set up. Included in the group were three administrators over the province of Babylon—Shadrach, Meshach, and Abednego.

Let's allow Daniel to tell it: "Then the herald loudly proclaimed, 'This is what you are commanded to do . . . : As soon as you hear the sound of the horn, flute, zither, lyre, harp, pipes and all kinds of music, you must fall down and worship the image of gold that King Nebuchadnezzar has set up. Whoever does not fall down and worship will immediately be thrown into a blazing furnace' " (Daniel 3:4-6).

Talk about intimidating!

You know what happens. These three stand their ground. Literally. They stand. They don't bow.

Furious with rage, their boss, Nebuchadnezzar, summoned the three to hear his threat renewed. "If you are ready to fall down and worship the image I made, very good." In other words: "The misunderstanding on your part will be overlooked. I mean, you've been loyal employees. But if you do not worship the image, you will be thrown into a blazing furnace. Then what god will be able to rescue you from my hand?"

The response of Shadrach, Meshach, and Abednego is classic. It captures where all of us need to be: "O Nebuchadnezzar, we do not need to defend ourselves before you in this matter. If we are thrown into the blazing furnace, the God we serve is able to save us from it, and he will rescue us from your hand, O king. But even if he does not, we want you to know, O king, that we will not serve your gods or worship the image of gold you have set up" (vv. 16-18).

Nebuchadnezzar was not a happy man. He was furious "and his attitude toward [the three men] changed. He ordered the furnace heated seven times hotter than usual. . . . the furnace [was] so hot that the flames of the fire killed the soldiers" who threw the three Hebrews into the furnace (vv. 19, 22).

Nevertheless, Shadrach, Meshach, and Abednego lived—which probably surprised them as much as it did the king! I'm sure they were ready to pay the ultimate price.

You know what? The experience of these men isn't unique. Different versions have been happening for years. And it's because such experiences are not uncommon that we wrote the Ultimate Authority Prayer. We designed the prayer to be prayed every day during this fifty-day spiritual adventure so it would become almost second nature. That way, whenever someone begins to play music that conflicts with the desires of your Lord, the issue will already have been settled.

But let's return to our three courageous friends. Listen to Daniel 3:24-25: "Then King Nebuchadnezzar leaped to his feet in amazement and asked his advisers, 'Weren't there three men that we tied up and threw into the fire?' They replied, 'Certainly, O king.' He said, 'Look! I see four men walking around in the fire, unbound and unharmed, and the fourth looks like a son of the gods.' "

Does anybody have any idea who that was? It's right there in our prayer: "The promise of your presence."

Accounts of believers who stand their ground when intimidated are always thrilling to read. Many of them come from times of revival in the church. I think of Martin Luther almost 470 years ago, being tried as a heretic at the Diet of Worms. He faced the real possibility of being burned at the stake, as Jan Hus had been earlier. Eventually it came down to whether he would recant his writings.

"Martin," said Eck, Luther's examiner, "answer candidly. Do you or do you not repudiate your books and the errors which they contain?"

Sweating because of the seriousness of the occasion, Luther replied, "Since then your majesty and your lordships desire a simple reply, I will answer without horns and without teeth. Unless I am convicted by Scripture and plain reason—I do not accept the authority of popes and councils, for they have contradicted each other—my conscience is captive to the word of God. I cannot, and I will not recant anything, for to go against conscience is neither right nor safe. Here I stand, I cannot do otherwise. God help me."[2]

What fire do you face in your work, my friend? Are you afraid of it? Intimidated? I don't blame you. But it can be overcome, just as Shadrach, Meshach, and Abednego learned. Stand tall for your Lord, and count on his presence in the midst of the flames.

> When through fiery trials thy pathway shall lie,
> My grace, all sufficient, shall be thy supply;
> The flame shall not hurt thee—
> I only design thy dross to consume
> and thy gold to refine.
>
> Fear not, I am with thee—O be not dismayed,
> For I am thy God, I will still give thee aid;
> I'll strengthen thee, help thee,
> and cause thee to stand,
> Upheld by my gracious, omnipotent hand.[3]

D.M.

End-of-the-Day Replay

1. Remove distractions

2. Rerun the events of your day

3. Respond to Christ's evaluation

I sensed Christ said to me:

"This was well done: _____

_____

_____."

"Work harder on this: _____

_____

_____."

☐ I am remembering this week to give away three of the presents of Christ and to record this information on page 120.

Resisting Temptation
Tuesday, Day Twenty-Four

Christ wants to transform my daily work. Through today's Scripture, 2 Timothy 3:12-17, he is saying to me specifically, "_____, in your work situation _____ _____." "

You may keep extremely busy in your daily work, but that doesn't mean you'll never be tempted. No matter where you go or what you're doing, sooner or later temptation comes calling. It's a part of daily work, whether you're a student, a salesperson, a publisher, a plumber, a riveter, or a retiree. If you don't give temptation an entrance, someone else will open the door.

That was the case with a handsome, well-built young man who had been entrusted with great responsibility by his boss. The boss's wife noticed the looks and build of our subject and propositioned him. Of course, I'm thinking about Joseph, whose story is found in Genesis.

I know Joseph wasn't familiar with the Ultimate Authority Prayer of this adventure, but it would have served him well. The daily, repeated reminders in that prayer—not only that we live in a two-boss world and that God is our ultimate authority, but that we are to resist temptation—are always timely.

Temptation is a powerful force. Maybe it's a sexual one, like Joseph faced—or the one you do. You never dreamed your affections could be captured by someone other than your mate. You were always very careful. But working closely with another person x-number of hours a week has opened you to new areas of interest, new experiences . . . to a strange, new closeness and an old temptation.

Or it's financial pressures, unexpected bills. You're getting further and further behind until now there's a danger of losing everything. Suddenly, you're vulnerable to considering what you never would have imagined before—taking what isn't yours. Stealing. Who would miss it? Who would even think you'd do such a thing? But, in a flash, it would solve your problem.

Temptation.

At times, the enemy almost seems more understanding than God. He's the one who seems to say, "Oh, yes, I can empathize. She really is beautiful. If you'd known her before you married, you certainly would have made a different choice. Life's far too short to have to live with all your mistakes. Go for it!"

Or, "Oh, it's not like taking money from a person. You're getting it out of a business. Besides, when you get ahead again, you can always put it back and then it's not stealing, is it? And think how good it will be to finally get those creditors off your back."

Or, "Face it, kid, cheat. Everybody does it. You're dumb not to. It means you're competing at an unfair advantage. Would you believe some of the kids in the class already know what the questions on the test will be before they even see it? So the little added help you're thinking about taking—it hardly even qualifies as cheating."

When you're under pressure, who's more sympathetic than Satan? But listen: As soon as you take the step, the moment you do what he's encouraging you to do, how quickly he changes his tune! Immediately it's, "You knew that was wrong before you did it, didn't you? What kind of Christian are you supposed to be?" "Cheating? Of course it's cheating. You'll never get by with it." "They'll discover the money's gone. Count on it happening." "How could you ever fall for that jerk? You were taken advantage of, you dope. But there's no way out now."

The poem says, "He makes a lash of your remembered sin, he weaves it firm and strong with cruel tip. And though your quivering flesh shrinks from scourge, with steady arm he plies the ruthless whip." A whip spelled G-U-I-L-T.

How much better to regularly remind ourselves of God's will, to tell ourselves that following him is the wisest of ways. To pray, "Help me to please you today, Christ, by resisting temptation."

Joseph's bottom line was that he saw himself ultimately responsible to God. Here's how the text puts it: "Now Joseph was well-built and handsome, and after a while his master's wife took notice of Joseph and said, 'Come to bed with me!' But he refused. 'With me in charge,' he told her, 'my master does not concern himself with anything in the house. . . . My master has withheld nothing from me except you, because you are his wife. How then could I do such a wicked thing and sin against my boss, your husband?' " (Genesis 39:6-9).

I changed something. Did you catch it? What Joseph really said was, "How then could I do such a wicked thing and sin *against God*?"—his other boss, if you please.

Sometimes making the Lord boss number one can get you into trouble with boss number two. Ask Joseph!

The story continues: "Though she spoke to Joseph day after day, he refused to go to bed with her or even be with her" (v. 10). But she was persistent. "One day he went into the house to attend to his duties, and none of the household servants was inside. She caught him by his cloak and said, 'Come to bed with me!' But he left his cloak in her hand and ran out of the house" (vv. 11-12).

You can believe she had quite a grip on that cloak! What a temptation for a young man! The more he refused, the more she wanted him. Finally Joseph had to flee. Even then he landed in jail, because the woman lied to her husband: " 'That Hebrew slave you brought us came to me to make sport of me. But as soon as I screamed for help, he left his cloak beside me and ran out of the house.' When his master heard the story . . . , he burned with anger. . . . and put [Joseph] in prison, the place where the king's prisoners were confined" (vv. 17-20).

God sure gives great rewards for righteousness, doesn't he? Do you ever feel that way? "The devil gives all the prizes! The Lord apparently doesn't believe in that system unless it concerns the life to come."

I'm sure Joseph wouldn't agree with what I just wrote. He would insist that if you're interested in rewards, following the Lord is the best course. It was for him. Before long, he enjoyed a position of power, wealth, prestige, and a long, long life.

Read his story in the remaining chapters of Genesis and you'll agree. If Christ is to transform our daily work, it's mandatory that we learn to resist temptation.

The lesson here is simple. If you want Joseph-sized rewards, you've got to follow a Joseph-style life.

D.M.

End-of-the-Day Replay

1. Remove distractions

2. Rerun the events of your day

3. Respond to Christ's evaluation

I sensed Christ said to me:

"This was well done: _____

_____

_____."

"Work harder on this: _____

_____

_____."

☐ I remembered to pray the Ultimate Authority Prayer today.

God Owns This Business

Wednesday, Day Twenty-Five

Christ wants to transform my daily work. Through today's Scripture, Daniel 3:13-18, he is saying to me specifically,
"_____, *in your work situation*
_____
_____. "

—

DAVID: Stanley Tam is an active businessman from Lima, Ohio, even though he is in his mid-seventies. He wrote a fascinating book called *God Owns My Business*, with more than 300,000 copies in print. Mr. Tam, what kind of business is it that God owns?

STANLEY: We manufacture industrial plastics and sell it to industries all over the United States and the world. Our company now covers five acres under one roof. We make about 111,000 shipments a year.

DAVID: That's a lot of plastic! Tell me about the ownership arrangement that you and God have worked out.

STANLEY: In the early days, I went broke in this business. Coming back from Columbus to get another job, I was praying to God about my disappointment. As I was praying, God spoke to my heart and said, "Stanley, it doesn't need to be a disappointment. You don't need to go broke in your business. Turn it over to me, and I'll make it succeed." That day I made God a covenant. I said,

"God, if you'll take this business and make it succeed, I will honor you in any way I possibly can."

I came home, had a talk with my dad, and convinced him that he should stake me financially again. He did, and I started out. God kept his part. In 1940, as the business grew, we went to a lawyer and made God our senior partner. We incorporated our business, issued stock, and then incorporated as a non-profit religious foundation. Then we gave the stock as a gift to the foundation. Whoever owns the stock owns the business.

DAVID: What kind of annual profits is the Lord getting out of this business?

STANLEY: For many years now, it's been about $1.5 million. We invest most of it in foreign missions.

DAVID: And what do you do, Mr. Tam? Do you take a salary?

STANLEY: Yes, since 1955.

DAVID: Did you write your book so that other businesspeople could copy what you're doing?

STANLEY: It's an inspirational, motivational book. I get a lot of help by reading biographies of men God has used like Charles Kraft of the Kraft Cheese Company, or Henry Crowe of the Quaker Oats Company. I think these books give men ideas—"Hey, I could trust God for something, too."

DAVID: You say that one of your guideposts in life is to pay any price necessary in order to be obedient to the Holy Spirit. Has the Holy Spirit made demands on you from time to time?

STANLEY: Yes. I'll pay any price in time, money, self, and pride, to be in a place where God can use me. That's where my power is. If anything is accomplished through my life, it's in complete surrender to the Holy Spirit.

Once I had to make restitution to the inventor of a product we sell. I took a trip to Wilmington, Delaware, and I told him I'd sinned against him and that I'd come to make restitution. I knew the only restitution he was interested in was financial. I told him that I had come to see if we could come to an agreement within my means to pay. We spent about a day and finally agreed that if I would pay him so many thousands of dollars, he would forgive me for breaking the contract. So I paid him that amount.

DAVID: There's a huge sign on the main building of your extremely large complex. What is that sign?

STANLEY: It says, "Christ is the answer." We build our business on Matthew 6:33: "Seek ye first the kingdom of God and his righteousness, and all these things shall be added unto you." We put "Christ is the answer" on the building for people who go by. We're right on Interstate 75, and statistics show 500,000 people a week go past our building.

One day a tractor-trailer broke down out front. The truck driver came in to use our telephone. I met him in the lobby and asked, "What's your problem?" He said his crankshaft had broken and the wrecker couldn't come for two hours. "Did you see the sign on my building?" I asked. He said he had, and I asked if he'd like to talk about it. "I've got two hours," he replied.

Later in my office, he got down on his knees and accepted Christ. When he got up, he said, "My wife is a Christian, and she's been praying for me. A friend of mine sat me down in a chair three weeks ago and pleaded with me to give my life to Christ." "Have you got a testimony!" I said. "Here's your wife praying for you, your friend is praying for you, and you're running away from God. But your truck breaks down right in front of the sign that says 'Christ is the answer'."

DAVID: You've also shown me two large catalogs, almost the size of phone books. Everything is normal about these plastic catalogs except the inside front cover. Tell me about that.

STANLEY: We use it to give our testimony and to talk about my book. We like to sell our book to unsaved men. So far, 2,495 people have received Christ through the book. We also advertise our motion picture. We say, "Show this to twenty-five people or more at your factory, and we'll send the film to you complimentary." We've heard of many conversion experiences through the film. Also, for forty-eight years now, we have put a gospel portion in our shipments. Last year, 664 of our customers wrote us to say they had prayed to receive Christ as Savior because of these gospel portions.

DAVID: Didn't you also begin Bible classes in your company?

STANLEY: Yes. To date, 109 people have come to know Christ as Savior through the Bible classes.

135

DAVID: People might say, "Well, you're an exceptional salesman." But don't you say that by nature you're shy?

STANLEY: The greatest soul winners are introverts because they trust the Holy Spirit. The Holy Spirit is the true soul winner. He does the convicting, he does the saving, he does the keeping. As we become master-controlled, like Romans 12:1 says—"Present your body a living sacrifice"—the will of God will be performed. And the will of God is that none should perish. As we surrender our lives to him, he'll win souls through us. This past ten days we've seen seven people come to our plant to receive Christ as Savior. They've come from all over the United States. They drive in, fly in, whatever.

DAVID: And the story goes on!

End-of-the-Day Replay

1. Remove distractions

2. Rerun the events of your day

3. Respond to Christ's evaluation

I sensed Christ said to me:

"This was well done: _____

_____

_____."

"Work harder on this: _____

_____

_____."

☐ I have given away at least one of the presents of Christ this week and have recorded this information on page 120.

God Owns This Business, II

Thursday, Day Twenty-Six

Christ wants to transform my daily work. Through today's Scripture, Matthew 6:24, he is saying to me specifically, "_____, in your work situation _____ _____."

DAVID: Mr. Tam, let's talk about prayer partnerships, or building strong supportive relationships with other Christians. Tell me about your support relationship with a man called Art.

STANLEY: Many years ago, a representative for Inter-Varsity came to see me. In the course of conversation he said, "Mr. Tam, do you have any friends?" I said, "Well, yes, I have a lot of friends." He said, "Do you have one, true friend?" I said, "What are you driving at?" "Suppose you fell into sin or you had an accident or you went broke in your business. Do you have a friend that would stick with you through thick and thin?" I said, "Well, maybe I don't have a friend like that."

"Well," he said, "there's a movement going across America, where a man like you would have a prayer partner. You would meet at least once a week to pray. You know, Mr. Tam, you have a weak point in your Christian life. I don't know what it is, but every Christian has a weak point. And that's where Satan will always attack. It may be a temper, it may be resentment, it may be fear or doubt, but you have a weakness. When you have a prayer partner, your weakness will probably be his strength."

So I called up Art Arthur, a Christian businessman here in Lima, and challenged him to become my prayer partner. He said, "Tam, I'll make a covenant with you for one year." Just recently we renewed this covenant for the twenty-sixth time. For twenty-six years, we have met once a week for one hour in the city park, and there we pray. I pray for his wife, his four children, and their families; he prays for my wife and four children and their families. I pray for his business; he prays for mine.

DAVID: What's happened as a result of all those years of praying?

STANLEY: Amazingly, the Lord has kept our families safe. We also pray for others and put tract racks in laundromats in our vicinity. We've had as many as twenty-one laundromats with tract racks. More than two million gospel tracts have been taken now. My name and phone number appear on the bottom of the tract.

One night when I came home my wife said, "A man's going to call you real soon." When he called, he said, "I've got to see you tonight." "I'll be free at 9:30," I told him. When I met him, he said, "I have marital problems, so I've been doing my own laundry. For four months I've been reading those gospel tracts on North Kohl Street. Today I made a decision to give my life to Christ." Some years we see about twenty-five decisions.

DAVID: Do you have any advice for those who want to establish a support relationship with another Christian?

STANLEY: It should be a man with a man and a woman with a woman, a teenager with a teenager. You shouldn't pray for the whole world. Just center in on your families and on ministry. I believe my business has grown and so has Art's because of this prayer covenant.

DAVID: Has your prayer relationship with Art encouraged you to share your faith with others? Are you praying for specific people as you meet together in that park?

STANLEY: Yes. Art and I pray for the unsaved. I pray for his ministry, he prays for mine. One time a church just thirty miles north of here invited me to come and speak. It's one of those great cathedral-type churches, beautiful glass windows, but so cold spiritually. When the day came for me to go, the weather was so bad I hesitated. It was freezing and everything was a sheet of ice. I said to my wife, "Honey, before I call them and tell them I can't come, maybe I ought to try it."

I was slipping and sliding but still making progress, so I decided to keep going. A great burden came upon my heart for a lost soul. When I got there, not many people had showed up—fifty, sixty people. After I spoke, nobody wanted to talk. The weather was so bad they all wanted to get home. So I put on my hat and coat, walked outside, and the janitor locked the door behind me. Now it was snowing on top of the ice. As I walked across the parking lot to my automobile, I met a lady who stopped me. "Mr. Tam, I just want to thank you for coming in such bad weather." She stopped, then blurted out, "But personally, I'm not happy you came tonight." "Lady, why aren't you happy I came?" I asked. "Oh, that talk you gave. 'If you were to die tonight, where would you go?' I know where I'm going, and it's not to heaven."

What do you do in a parking lot at 9:30 at night with a lady who has a spiritual problem and they've locked up the church? Do you say to her, "Well, lady, I've got thirty miles to go, so I'd better get going. Good night. Hope you get to heaven!" That's not the answer. So what do you do? Do you say, "Well, over here's my car. Let's go talk about it." I'm a married man, she's a married woman, and that's not good Christian ethics. What do you do? You do what you're supposed to. You ask the Holy Spirit, the true soul winner, what to do. In that moment, he gave me direction. I said, "Lady, where's your husband?" "Oh, he's over here in the car waiting for me." I asked, "What does he think about it?" "He's as upset as I am." "Alright, invite me over to your house tonight." "Oh, no, I wouldn't do that." "Why not?" "Oh, Mr. Tam, look at the weather! You've got thirty miles to go on this ice and snow. I'd never invite you to my house tonight."

But if you're a soul winner, that doesn't stop you. I insisted, and soon she said, "OK." I followed them home, and when I walked into their house I discovered why I had a burden for a lost soul. She went in and grabbed a whole stack of letters from Christian broadcasters. "We've read these," she said, "but we don't know what to do to get peace in our hearts." "I can help you," I said. We took out our Bibles and I answered questions. I've never met a couple that had so many questions. But at midnight, they were on their knees, accepting Christ as their Savior. I've been back in that home many, many times, and they are beautiful Christians today.

The Bible abounds with God's invitation for us to involve him in the details of our lives. The satanic deceit is for man to relegate God to organ preludes and stained-glass windows and profound liturgies. Listen, God wants to be personal in our lives. I talk to him as I go to work. In every interview, every piece of business, I ask God to give me his mind so that I can have divine wisdom and divine knowledge to make divine decisions. The same can be true of anybody who's willing.

End-of-the-Day Replay

1. Remove distractions

2. Rerun the events of your day

3. Respond to Christ's evaluation

I sensed Christ said to me:

"This was well done: _____

_____

_____."

"Work harder on this: _____

_____

_____."

☐ I have established a support relationship with another Christian and am meeting at least once a week.

A Classic Relationship

Friday, Day Twenty-Seven

Christ wants to transform my daily work. Through today's Scripture, Exodus 18:17-23, he is saying to me specifically,
"_____, *in your work situation*

_____

_____."

One of the things I've always loved about Scripture is the glimpses it gives us into human personalities and relationships. The biblical style is so direct. The good and bad qualities of each person are exposed, often without comment, thus leaving it up to the reader to draw conclusions and make application. In my thinking, this contributes to the Bible's "classic" style. Every generation of believer has been able to draw conclusions from the basic stories—conclusions which fit their particular era.

For example, Scripture never uses the words *support relationship*, a concept which seems particularly relevant to this generation which so often suffers from feelings of isolation and detachment. Finding someone to whom we can commit and have that commitment returned is a twentieth century felt need.

Although Scripture doesn't directly talk about support relationships, the concept is there nevertheless, tucked between factual accounts. By observing the uniquely positive relationship between Moses and Jethro described in Exodus 18:17-23, for example, we can discover helpful insights into building positive support relationships.

First let's examine the biblical account. After fleeing from Egypt to Midian, Moses found favor with Jethro, priest of Midian, when he protected the priest's daughters from shepherds who had driven the sisters from a well. This kindness won him a wife and a position in the family business as a sheep herder. So for years, Jethro was not only Moses' father-in-law, but his boss.

At the time our account begins, Moses had already led Israel out of Egypt. Without explanation, Scripture states that Moses had sent his wife, Zipporah, and his two sons back to her father. But while Moses camped with Israel in the desert, Jethro brought Moses' family back to him.

Moses must have been thrilled to see his family and his old friend again. He had a lot to tell them. He described all the things God had done for Israel's sake, how they had been rescued from their enemies at the Red Sea. Jethro reacted by praising Israel's God, declaring him to be greater than all the other gods. Jethro then brought a burnt sacrifice and other offerings to God.

What can we learn about support relationships from Moses and Jethro so far? First, there was a spiritual element to their relationship. They shared a common outlook on life which viewed God as actively involved in their affairs. Worship and praise were natural reactions for these men. They were able to see beyond the physical details of life to the spiritual dimension.

That's the way it is with the best of support relationships. People involved in support relationships get beyond surface talk in order to spend time praying and talking about how God is working in each other's lives. This interest and outlook draws people close as they rejoice and praise God for his direction, evidences of love, and care.

But even the best relationship can get tricky at times. That's the second thing we notice in the relationship between Jethro and Moses. Scripture says the next day Moses took his seat to serve as judge for the people, who stood around him from morning until evening. Jethro saw this job was too much for Moses and offered some constructive criticism and advice.

"What you are doing is not good," he told Moses. "You and these people . . . will only wear yourselves out. The work is too heavy for you; you cannot handle it alone. Listen now to me and I will give you some advice.... Select capable men ... who fear God, ... who hate dishonest gain. Appoint them as officials over thousands, hundreds, fifties and tens. Have them serve as judges for the people at all times, but have them bring every difficult case to you .... That will make your load lighter, because they will share it with you. If you do this ..., you will be able to stand the strain, and all these people will go home satisfied" (Exodus 18:17-19, 21-23).

At one time Jethro was the older man, the father-in-law, the boss; but things had changed. Moses was now the God-chosen leader of an entire nation. Jethro took a chance pointing out Moses' mistake. Dare you offer constructive criticism to a national hero who had just delivered a nation from its enemies and brought water from a rock? Yes, if there is enough mutual give-and-take in a relationship. Why did he do it? Perhaps he thought that Moses would have done the same for him.

To make support relationships work there must be give and take, giving and receiving. Both must be willing to exchange roles as the need arises and be either the advisor or the one receiving advice.

If most of a relationship is spent around one person's problems and needs, if all the gift-giving and card-sending only goes one way, then you do not have a support relationship, but a ministry! If someone does all the taking, then the person is not a friend, but a mission field!

On the other hand, if you will not surrender the role of advice-giver, if you never open up and share your personal struggles, if you continually insist on being the superior and refuse to be criticized or given advice, then you are not really a friend, but a surrogate parent!

Nothing threatens a friendship more than the lack of giving and receiving. A support relationship can survive the times you stick your foot in your mouth, or your minor personality quirks, or many other things, so long as the relationship is built on a shared spiritual outlook and a mutuality of relating.

Moses was a fortunate man. He listened to his father-in-law's advice. He did as Jethro had suggested ... and it worked!

And then matter-of-factly Scripture says, "Then Moses sent his father-in-law on his way, and Jethro returned to his own country." We're not told what they said to each other in parting. We're not told how they felt about leaving each other. We can only suppose that it was time for each man to get on with his own life, to get on with the job God had given each of them to do. But I think it would be fair to say that in the years of separation ahead of them, they would miss each other very much, and remember each other fondly.

That's how it is with support relationships. I can't fill in the details of how this might look in your life, but I can promise you that if you find a support relationship that works, no matter what life brings your way, you will become a better and wiser person. And even if life separates you, you will remember fondly the time spent together worshiping and praying, giving and receiving. And in the meantime, like Moses and Jethro, you may find that a good support relationship might just make all the difference in how you fare in those rough spots along the way.

V.B.

End-of-the-Day Replay

1. Remove distractions

2. Rerun the events of your day

3. Respond to Christ's evaluation

I sensed Christ said to me:

"This was well done: _____

_____

_____."

"Work harder on this: _____

_____

_____."

☐ This week I gave away three presents of Christ and recorded this information on page 120.

A Kick in the Side

Saturday, Day Twenty-Eight

Christ wants to transform my daily work. Through today's Scripture, Hebrews 10:19-25, he is saying to me specifically, "_____, *in your work situation* _____ _____ ."

_____

Very often, God chooses to work in our lives through other believers. One to one, we can help each other through the delights and the dilemmas of our daily work.

That doesn't mean, of course, that people will never let us down. I've been burned. I've expected to be encouraged and supported, and instead found I was being undermined behind my back. That's painful. But at the same time, some of the most potent spiritual lessons I've learned have come through supportive relationships.

Take praying, for example. I've read books on praying and have heard sermons on the subject. They're all helpful, but I've learned more about praying by simply listening to others pray. Or take witnessing. I've learned immense lessons by watching others as they witness, and I've thought, *I could do that, too!*

Support relationships in which we spur on each other to accelerated spiritual growth—that's the idea in Hebrews 10:19-25. I think particularly of verse 24, where we're told, "And let us consider how we may spur one another on toward love and good deeds."

Whenever I hear that verse, I think of an incident when I was young. I was sitting on a horse and couldn't get it to move. "Kick the horse in the side!" I was told. I was a little hesitant—I didn't want to kick it real hard because I thought I would be in big trouble if he took off. But soon I found that a little boy in gym shoes can kick a horse *very* hard, and still he isn't going to budge. A spur would have helped.

That's what I think of here. We want a spiritual growth spurt, so a kick in the side will be helpful. That's what a supportive relationship does.

Verse 25 goes on to say, "Let us not give up meeting together, as some are in the habit of doing, but let us encourage one another . . . . " While we often think of the need to be in church, there's also the idea of getting together in a one-on-one basis. Just being in a corporate worship service or in a Sunday school class does not necessarily mean we're getting all the support we need.

It's also important that they be the "right" one-on-one relationships. I may not be much help to some folks. If a bus driver says, "Here are my pressures, help me with these," I may not be able to identify with him. Maybe a high schooler comes, and it's been a long time since I was in high school. I'm probably not the one to help him. Or a grade schooler. Could you help a grade schooler? Maybe you could because of your children, but still it's hard to get back into that world. I say to myself, "How in the world can I relate to this individual?" The relationship has to be with the right person.

If we would look back on some of the relationships where we have been burned, probably it's been because the other person lacked the capacity to understand our unique pressures. It just wasn't the right match. We tried to force something that wasn't natural.

My own experience has been exciting of late because I now have a wonderful relationship. I asked myself, "What are the unique pressures I face? Who in my church can identify with those problems? Who struggles with trying to keep the money coming in to match a growing budget? Who does fund-raising? And who can identify with the pressure of constant deadlines?"

The person I found owns his own television company. I had to find somebody who headed his business, who could identify with trying to encourage his employees, but who maybe didn't have a peer to encourage him. I found that person, and it wasn't the pastor. My pastor is marvelous, but many of the pressures I face are outside his field of experience. It's been great to approach this friend and say, "Hey, could I talk over some of the problems I face as a Christian in my work setting, and see if you could help me from your perspective?" It's been absolutely marvelous.

Do you want to quicken your spiritual pace? Then build a relationship with a fellow Christian who understands the unique pressures of your work world.

To try to take the bigness out of this job and bring it down to simplicity, first we need to identify the pressures in our own worlds. What are the kinds of things that are unique to me, that most people would not understand? How does my faith impinge upon my work life? Perhaps some of the pressures will be feelings of guilt—maybe real guilt because I know I'm not living for Christ the way I could. Write these things down.

Second, after you've identified your pressures, begin to think of someone in your congregation who would understand them. Then pray about it. Don't just identify someone who quickly comes to mind, but as the Lord leads, look for someone who could lend a sympathetic ear, an understanding spirit, someone with whom you feel comfortable in conversation.

Third, I suggest you go to that person and say, "I've had some struggles at work as they relate to my faith; I'm not sure I'm doing as well as I could. I've been praying about this, and I wondered if I could talk with you. Here are the kind of things I have in mind," and then you share what some of those problems are. "Would it be possible sometime for me to sit down with you and see what you do in this area?"

I have a feeling the reply will be, "Hey, I struggle with those things, too. I may not have all of the answers, but I'd be more than happy to talk about it. And thank you for asking." Then the relationship has the opportunity to grow into something even more beneficial in the days ahead.

That kind of approach sets up a short-term relationship. It might be just one conversation, and that in itself could be helpful. But if you find this becomes mutually helpful, it could grow and go on and on. And that could be wonderful.

147

I know this might sound intimidating, but be encouraged. Take the step. It's not a huge thing. I'm not asking you to bargain away the whole of your life or your faith. Just move forward, reach out, and see what happens.

It may be that you'll see the pace quickened in your spiritual life. It's like that horse I tried to ride as a child—until you've been on a horse that gallops, you haven't known true excitement. But hold on to that neck! It's a whole new world. You're going forward! And that's what we want. That's what we've promised in this adventure.

Experience it, my friend!

D.M., S.B.

End-of-the-Day Replay

1. Remove distractions

2. Rerun the events of your day

3. Respond to Christ's evaluation

I sensed Christ said to me:

"This was well done: _____

_____

_____."

"Work harder on this: _____

_____

_____."

☐ I remembered to pray the Ultimate Authority Prayer today.

Week Four Notes

1. Jack Eckerd and Charles P. Conn, *Eckerd: Finding the Right Prescription* (Old Tappan, N.J.: Fleming H. Revell, 1987), pp. 187-90.

2. Roland H. Bainton, *Here I Stand* (Nashville: Abingdon Press, 1950), p. 185.

3. "How Firm a Foundation."

Build Strong, Supportive Relationships with Other Christians

Very often, God chooses to work in our lives
through other believers.
One to one, we can help each other
through the delights and dilemmas of our daily work.

Week Five:
Recording Progress

Bridge the Gap between Church and Work
(Details on page 13.)

To help bridge the church/work gap I completed assignment number _____ on _____(date). The experience taught me that _____

_____

_____

_____.

Delight Others by Giving Away the Presents of Christ
(Details on page 18.)

This week I tried to delight others by giving the presents of Christ three times in the following ways:

1. On _____ I gave a present of _____

    to _____.

2. On _____ I gave a present of _____

    to _____.

3. On _____ I gave a present of _____

    to _____.

True Power

Sunday, Day Twenty-Nine

Christ wants to transform my daily work. Through today's Scripture, Ecclesiastes 4:9-12, he is saying to me specifically,

"_____, *in your work situation*

_____

_____ ."

Power. What comes to mind when you hear that word? Sports fans might think of the offensive front line of the defending Super Bowl champions. For others, power is the deafening rocket blast that hurtles our astronauts into outer space. Power can be associated politically with a despot who rules with an iron hand. In the business world, maybe it's the financial tycoon who heads the conglomerate and is reputed to have a wastebasket into which he throws nothing but human beings!

Sometimes when we hear the term "spiritual power," we think of extremes as well. Can we learn to part the waters? To call fire down from heaven? To slay enemy troops with one fell stroke?

Not really.

In Scripture the word *power* relates to the advancement of the cause of Christ. In Acts chapter 1, Jesus says, "You will receive power when the Holy Spirit comes on you; and you will be my witnesses. . . . " So this power unleashed in the workplace is Christ using us as his presence.

153

So if you thought I was going to tell you how, through prayer, you could turn your boss into a toad, you're going to be disappointed. But if you want to know how to experience the wonder of Christ on Monday as well as Sunday, at work as well as worship, then listen closely to what follows.

In the spiritual realm, one plus one doesn't always equal two. When two or more are bonded in prayer, the spiritual result is far greater than the mere addition of a second or third person.

A young father was proud of his son, who was in first grade and was learning arithmetic. To show a visiting friend how smart the boy was, the man said to his son, "Johnny, you've been studying arithmetic. Tell me what one plus one is." There was a long, long pause. Finally the child, with a puzzled look, replied, "Daddy, I don't think we've gotten that far yet."

Sometimes I think this is the way we are in the church. We appear to know so much, when in truth we haven't even learned the primary lessons related to spiritual power. How much is one plus one in the spiritual realm? Let's just say it's equal to more than two.

For too long we've been praying alone. Too often we have opted for privacy at the loss of corporate power. What did the Lord say to us through Ecclesiastes 4:9-12? Here it is:

> Two are better than one, because they have a good return for their work: If one falls down, his friend can help him up. But pity the man who falls and has no one to help him up! Also, if two lie down together, they will keep warm. But how can one keep warm alone? Though one may be overpowered, two can defend themselves. A cord of three strands is not quickly broken.

And remember the words of Jesus himself:

> Where two or three are gathered together in My name, I am there in the midst of them (Matthew 18:20, NKJV).

How does this translate into the real world? It's an older dad and a married son who meet together early one morning every week to read Scripture and pray. It's a mother and her second-grade child going over what their day will be like, praying for each other before the child catches the school bus. It's a man going to his office early because he knows his friend two states away will call him to pray together for fifteen minutes about work-related matters and that the presence of Christ will be manifest in their lives.

It's two elected officials, sometimes on opposite sides of the legislative fence, getting together in each other's office on a rotating basis to pray that they will do their best in making decisions that will bring glory to the Lord. It's two believers getting together each Thursday noon in a tape manufacturing company to fast-lunch and bring before the Lord the names of friends at work who they trust someday will be touched by the beauty of Christ.

Are you beginning to grasp what spiritual power looks like? Believe me, it's a secret well worth knowing.

For too long, most of us have been content to go it alone. We need to learn the power of "one plus one equals more than two." To resist this truth is to forfeit the power that's needed to see the kingdom flag hoisted high over our work settings.

I can understand why you might be fearful, but I'm not encouraging you to make some huge commitment. To work on a support relationship for several weeks is not like asking you to marry someone. You're just saying, "Lord, with whom can I get together to share some of my concerns about work, to give perspective on how I'm doing in my walk with you, and, more than anything, to pray?"

Think about this. Try it for a month and make that the predetermined stopping point when you first get together. When you have a predetermined stopping time you'll be able to evaluate more easily whether the experience was beneficial.

When we build strong, supportive relationships with other Christians, we enable our Lord to infuse his presence more powerfully into our work settings.

Do you know what a bonus is? A bonus is something given beyond what's expected. If the bonus is of good size, you are pleased.

Let me promise you something. If you take me up on this challenge, I can practically guarantee you an enormous spiritual bonus. Its payoff will be much larger than anticipated, and the investment you make in establishing a support relationship will be small compared to the benefit you will receive.

That benefit will be for you . . . and for your Lord as well.

D.M.

End-of-the-Day Replay

1. Remove distractions
2. Rerun the events of your day
3. Respond to Christ's evaluation

I sensed Christ said to me:

"This was well done: _____

_____

_____."

"Work harder on this: _____

_____

_____."

☐ To bridge the church/work gap I have completed one of the weekly assignments and recorded this information on page 152.

A Rope of Sand

Monday, Day Thirty

Christ wants to transform my daily work. Through today's Scripture, Proverbs 19:20,27, he is saying to me specifically, "_____, in your work situation _____ _____."

Learning difficult new skills is intimidating for most of us. I know I am always a little hesitant in attempting something I've never done before. How about you?

Some people are marvelous skiers. I watch them in amazement. I've only skied once, and wouldn't have done it that often if other members of the family hadn't tried it with me. They seemed to make it easier. We could laugh about our mutual struggles and rejoice in our successes, as elementary as they were.

I bring this up because I know that for some people, the thought of accelerated spiritual growth is about as intimidating as being challenged to get involved in a fifty-day program that ends up with tryouts for the Olympic ski team!

The frightening part of this adventure is that we're talking about effectively living out our faith in the work setting, and that's one of the most difficult arenas. That's why the thought of having a Christian friend who's there to learn with us should be very appealing and comforting.

Revivalist John Wesley discovered this early on in his ministry. Wesley's name has been remembered better than that of his contemporary George Whitefield, even though back in the 1700s Whitefield was the better-known preacher.

One reason for this is discussed in Garth Lean's book about John Wesley, *Strangely Warmed.*

"Preaching like an apostle," said Wesley, "without joining together those who are awakened, and training them in the way of God, is only begetting children for the murderer. . . With no connections [or with no Christians teaming up with another], the consequence is that nine in ten of the once awakened are now faster asleep than ever."

Wesley's prediction was borne out in America. "There, tens of thousands of people had been converted under Whitefield's preaching. But Whitefield felt he had not the aptitude for founding and nurturing these societies. In consequence, many of Whitefield's converts faded away." Whitefield himself once described it as "weaving a rope of sand."

"Wesley, on the other hand," writes Lean, "grasped what was involved in winning, confirming, and setting men to work so that the nation would be 'reformed,' and he faced into the labor of doing the work necessary."[1]

These groups Wesley formed were characterized by complete honesty and complete trust in God and in each other. All members were pledged to secrecy regarding personal confessions. Questions were asked regularly, like, "Are you still studying Scripture? Are you overcoming temptation, and if not, why?"

In these smaller settings, "tens of thousands of ordinary men and women learned to take the further steps of change and thousands of leaders learned to lead. Class leaders were encouraged to make some report to Wesley himself every three months. . . and it was to visit these leaders, as well as to preach to the populace at large, that Wesley undertook his endless journeyings."

Wesley knew that one exposure to the gospel through preaching wasn't enough to establish the average person in the faith. For most converts, it requires more care, including growing along with others.

Earlier I said that learning new skills is intimidating for most people. On their own, most folks are hesitant to try something they've never before tried. *But working at it with a friend makes it a lot easier.*

Jesus knew this. What's a bigger assignment than to be told you're to change the world? That's what Christ commissioned his apostles to do. Their initial training came as part of a key group of twelve. Later they were sent out two by two. All through the book of Acts, two by two would remain the pattern.

But somewhere, between then and now, it's changed. In North America we tend to think people ought to be able to learn on their own how to pray, how to study the Scriptures, how to overcome temptation, or become good church members, or represent Christ in their daily work.

These are all hard disciplines. And some of them, like representing Christ in our daily work, can be extremely difficult.

So on this spiritual adventure we are encouraging you to find another who knows what it's like to work where you do. Someone who understands some of the tricky slopes, who perhaps has fallen down on occasion and can still feel the embarrassment. Someone who, maybe, has spiritually skied into a tree.

Have you found such a one to learn with you on this adventure? Have you looked for someone? Prayed about the possibility?

With no one to explore new areas with you, you'll probably not grow much beyond where you are now. That's not a very exciting prospect, is it? But with another to talk over your successes and failures, you may surprise yourself with your progress.

Would it be good for the church if we saw another sweeping revival as marked the era of John Wesley? Of course it would. What would it take for that to happen? Do we lack the preachers? I don't think so. North America is full of good preachers. But it takes more than preaching.

We have been too much like Whitefield and not enough like Wesley. In our evangelism, we, like Whitefield, have woven a rope of sand. We've counted too much on people learning through sermons and not enough on growth coming through supportive relationships. We've concentrated on Christ's preaching skills and failed to see his emphasis on small group discipling. We've talked too much about Paul and not enough about Paul and Barnabas or Paul and Silas or Paul and Timothy or Paul and a string of other names associated with his.

The rugged individualism that marks North Americans has been a cause for false pride when it comes to the church. All of us are much too independent, much too private. And because of this, we are much too immature.

What about you? Have you dismissed this idea of building a support relationship with another Christian? And if so, why?

I'm asking you to reconsider.

D.M.

End-of-the-Day Replay
1. Remove distractions
2. Rerun the events of your day
3. Respond to Christ's evaluation

I sensed Christ said to me:

"This was well done: _____

_____

_____."

"Work harder on this: _____

_____

_____."

☐ I am remembering this week to give away three of the presents of Christ and to record this information on page 152.

Two Are Better than One

Tuesday, Day Thirty-One

Christ wants to transform my daily work. Through today's Scripture, James 3:9-12, he is saying to me specifically,

"_____, *in your work situation*

_____

_____ ."

━━━━━
━━━━━

Let me introduce you to a pair of brave ladies whose names you probably don't know—Shiphrah and Puah. You probably aren't familiar with the two brave Smith sisters, either—Peggy and Christine. I'll tell you about them a little later.

Shiphrah and Puah were midwives. That has to be a tough job. To begin with, it's hard to schedule your work. You can't just say to a woman in labor, "Sorry, but it's 4:30. Time for me to leave. But I'll be back again tomorrow right at 8 A.M."

I also suspect midwifery was much harder before the era of modern medicine. I mention that because Shiphrah and Puah lived back in the years immediately following the patriarchs. Their names appear in Exodus 1, where we learn that the Hebrews were no longer as accepted in Egypt as they had been when Joseph was the number two official there. "The Egyptians came to dread the Israelites," the Bible says, and "they made their lives bitter with hard labor in brick and mortar and with all kinds of work in the fields; in all their hard labor the Egyptians used them ruthlessly."

161

Then follows the story of these two women who came to know firsthand just how ruthless the Egyptians could be. Exodus 1:15-16: "The king of Egypt said to the Hebrew midwives . . . , 'When you help the Hebrew women in childbirth and observe them on the delivery stool, if it is a boy, kill him. . . .' "

How's that for an awful assignment? Talk about a two-boss tension! These women had to contend with triple tension: a hard job; a boss who was ruthless; and now, a vile work order that violated their Hebrew belief about the sanctity of life.

Did you notice that I didn't say, "This woman," but rather, "These women"? I can't prove it, but I suspect it was an advantage to have each other's strength to draw upon. Shiphrah and Puah plotted their mutual defense.

"The midwives, however, feared God and did not do what the king of Egypt had told them to do; they let the boys live. Then the king of Egypt summoned the midwives [a frightening summons to receive, I'm sure!] and asked them, 'Why have you done this? Why have you let the boys live?'" There had to be some collusion here, because the two answered Pharaoh as one: "Hebrew women are not like Egyptian women; they are vigorous and give birth before the midwives arrive" (Exodus 1:17-19).

Caught in an ethical bind, they chose the lesser of the evils and lied rather than killed. Verses 20-21 read, "So God was kind to the midwives . . . and because the midwives feared God, he gave them families of their own."

Have you discovered Shiphrah and Puah's secret? Have you developed a friendship at your place of work with another who fears God? At your office? At your construction site? At your school? At your military base? At your restaurant?

In his book *Revival God's Way*, Leonard Ravenhill writes about two elderly sisters whose work was prayer. They were eighty-four and eighty-two—Peggy and Christine Smith. Peggy was blind and her sister was almost bent double with arthritis. But the Lord used these two women, who lived on islands off the west coast of Scotland, in what is now referred to as the "Hebrides Revival."

The then-famous Duncan Campbell had turned down an invitation to preach there and this had been accepted as the mind of the Lord by most. Peggy, however—the blind prayer warrior—

162

would have none of it. Ravenhill writes, "The second letter saying that Duncan Campbell could not come to the place brought this answer from her: 'That's what the *man* says—God has said otherwise! Write again! He will be here within a fortnight.' He went."

After Campbell had preached on the foolish virgins and come down from the pulpit, a young deacon raised his hand and, moving it in a circle over his head, said, "Mr. Campbell, God is hovering over: I can hear already the rumbling of heaven's chariot wheels."

The entire congregation was lingering outside the church. Many faces showed signs of deep spiritual distress. Suddenly a young man, overburdened for the lost around him, broke out in an agonizing cry—his prayer a flame! . . The congregation moved back into the church. Many sought the Lord. There was great grief over and repentance for sin. Now the revival was on.

While the Lord was working in the church building, Peggy and her sister were interceding at the throne. Peggy sent the following message to her minister—"We struggled through the hours of the night refusing to take a denial. Had He not promised, and would He not fulfill? . . . . Did He fail us? Never! Before the morning light broke, we *saw* the enemy retreating, and our wonderful Lamb take the field."

. . . Yes, there is a word that says, "Touch not mine anointed, and do my prophets no harm." But what if the prophet is temporarily out of hearing of the Lord? Andrew Woolsey, the biographer of Duncan Campbell, talked of Peggy's having a holy intimacy with the Lord. How right he is. Paul said, "I withstood [Peter] to the face." Peggy withstood Campbell. She had asked the preacher to come to a small, isolated village and hold a meeting. The people of that village were not in favor of revival-type meetings, Duncan told Peggy so, and that he doubted her wisdom in this thing. She turned in the direction of his voice, her sightless eyes seeming to penetrate his soul, and said, "Mr. Campbell, if you were living as near to God as you ought to be, He would reveal His secrets to you also."

Duncan accepted the rebuke. Then he knelt with Peggy, and the dear intercessor said, "Lord, You remember what You told me this morning, that in this village You are going to save seven men who will be pillars in the church of my fathers. Lord, I have given Your message to

Mr. Campbell, and he seems not prepared to accept it. O Lord, give him wisdom, because he badly needs it."

Duncan Campbell went to the village, preaching in the large room of a house. His message was, "The times of this ignorance God winked at: but now commandeth all men everywhere to repent." By the time he was through preaching, many were mourning for their sins among them Peggy's seven men.[2]

Shiphrah and Puah. Peggy and Christine. And what's your name? What's the name of the person who supports you in your adventures of faith?

It's easier to be spiritually brave when you have such a one. So if you don't have one, find one. You'll be amazed at the results.

D.M.

End-of-the-Day Replay

1. Remove distractions

2. Rerun the events of your day

3. Respond to Christ's evaluation

I sensed Christ said to me:

"This was well done: _____

_____

_____."

"Work harder on this: _____

_____

_____."

☐ I remembered to pray the Ultimate Authority Prayer today.

A Pearl for Pressured Workers

Wednesday, Day Thirty-Two

Christ wants to transform my daily work. Through today's Scripture, Proverbs 17:17, he is saying to me specifically,

"_____, *in your work situation*

_____

_____."

When your work puts you under pressure, when things go wrong, how do you respond? Do you complain? Get grumpy? Short tempered? Get down on yourself and worry about it? Get depressed? Question whether you still have what it takes to get the job done? Perhaps you even want out. I'm sure there are times when you wonder, *Am I going to make it?*

I have a suggestion that might make all the difference. If you follow through on it, you may be thanking me for years to come. Here it is:

It's easier to make the best of a tough work situation when you go through it with somebody else.

Sound too simple? The idea isn't mine. It comes right out of Scripture in Ecclesiastes 4:9-10, where we're told that "Two are better than one, because . . . if one falls down, his friend can help him up." Verse 10 concludes: "But pity the man who falls and has no one to help him up!"

Maybe up to this point you've been alone in your daily work-place—if not literally, at least emotionally. There's no one with whom you can share your frustrations, your insecurities . . . especially when things go wrong. The fact is, in some situations, such a conversation could jeopardize your job.

This support person may or may not work with you. What's important is that each of us needs someone with whom we can honestly discuss what's happening in our lives—and a major chunk of our lives revolves around daily work.

A couple of days ago I was talking to a pastor-friend. He told me that building support relationships was one of the most significant factors in his congregation's spiritual growth. He regularly hears his people say things like, "Meeting regularly with another person interested in my world is one of the best things that has ever happened to me. The benefits are mutual."

An illustration of this comes from Acts 16. Paul and Silas had joined together for a preaching tour to plant churches among the Gentiles. Their daily work consisted of traveling, meeting new people, and sharing the gospel at every opportunity.

They ran into trouble when they arrived in Philippi. A fortune-telling slave girl followed them for several days, making such a commotion that they weren't able to do their work. Paul became so frustrated that finally he turned around and said to the evil spirit in the girl, "In the name of Jesus Christ, I command you to come out of her!"

It did.

When the owners of the slave girl realized that their hope of making money from her was gone, they had Paul and Silas arrested. Now things really got tough. The authorities ordered Paul and Silas to be stripped and beaten and thrown into prison. Then they were placed in a maximum security cell and their feet were fastened in the stocks.

I doubt any of us have suffered anything like this on the job. It's a pretty tough work situation. But note what happens.

"About midnight Paul and Silas were praying and singing hymns to God, and the other prisoners were listening to them" (Acts 16:25).

Wait a minute! It's not supposed to work this way, is it?

Yes, it is. Back to Ecclesiastes 4: "Two are better than one," and "though one may be overpowered, two can defend themselves." In other words, two at least have a fighting chance in tough situations.

You know how the story goes. Not only did Paul and Silas benefit from their mutual support, there was a spillover effect that benefited the prisoners around them. Before the night was over, the Philippian jailer and his entire household became Christians because of these two.

Paul and Silas made it through this difficult work situation by going though it together. It was made bearable and produced positive results beyond anyone's wildest imagination.

Believers need each other, especially in the workplace. God never intended us to go it alone. There's no place in the kingdom for the lonesome, cowboy Christian.

Yesterday morning I met with one of my support persons. During our conversation over breakfast, I expressed feelings of personal frustration. I admitted how last week I hadn't been as productive as I had hoped. I was down on myself, discouraged, under pressure.

Suddenly he piped up, "Hey, snap out of it! Don't be so hard on yourself. You broke your ankle several weeks ago. You lost a week of work. You're still in a cast. Your whole system's been thrown off. If your expectations were more in line with reality, you wouldn't be so blue. Just focus on what needs to be done today, stay at it, then don't sweat it."

That was exactly what I needed to hear. This guy picked me up when I was down and put into words the perspective I lacked. I believe he told me the very thoughts of Jesus.

Sound farfetched? It isn't. It was Jesus himself who said, "Where two or three come together in my name, I am right there with them."

Listen: Building a support relationship not only makes it easier to make the best of a tough work situation, it's also another specific way Christ can make himself known to you. He wants you to keep life in perspective. And I know that's what you want, too. Right?

So keep at it! Build a supportive relationship with another Christian. You'll both be better for it. And who knows? Like Paul and Silas, the positive spillover may go beyond your wildest imagination.

S.B.

End-of-the-Day Replay

1. Remove distractions

2. Rerun the events of your day

3. Respond to Christ's evaluation

I sensed Christ said to me:

"This was well done: _____

_____

_____."

"Work harder on this: _____

_____

_____."

☐ I have given away at least one of the presents of Christ this week and have recorded this information on page 152.

Rest, Then Work

Thursday, Day Thirty-Three

Christ wants to transform my daily work. Through today's Scripture, Matthew 6:19-21, he is saying to me specifically, "_____, *in your work situation* _____ _____ ." "

DAVID: Ben Patterson is a Presbyterian pastor in New Jersey, and the author of a book about work and worship called *The Grand Essentials*. Ben, you say there's a time for work and a time for rest. How are work and rest related?

BEN: Biblically, we start with rest and move to work, and not the other way around. We tend to see rest as the reward we give ourselves for all the work we do. But biblically, we start with rest. The prime example of this is when the day begins, according to a biblical reckoning of time. It begins with sundown. Read the Genesis account of creation. Each day begins with sundown. For the Jew, the Sabbath begins with sundown. And a remarkable thing happens when each day begins. What do you do? You go to bed. Then all night, you sleep. God runs the universe, he takes care of you, you get up in the morning, and you begin your day with most of it already having taken place.

169

It's just like our salvation. It's by grace we have been saved, not works. We don't work to earn God's grace. We start with grace and proceed to work.

DAVID: You say, "It's only as we learn to worship well that we truly learn to work well." Is this that reverse pattern again?

BEN: Yes. It's in the sanctuary, on the Lord's day, that our work is informed and transformed and that we gain the vision of life we must have if we're going to live biblically.

Worship is to the rest of our lives what the cultivation of a garden is to the rest of its life. You don't cultivate a garden all the time, but at signal moments, regularly and frequently, you weed it and fertilize it and prune it and water it. Worship is that way to the rest of our lives. Regularly and at signal moments we need to stop and cultivate our lives in worship.

DAVID: Our culture seems out of step with that. Old timers tell me that Sabbath observance has changed. Do you agree?

BEN: I certainly do. As one person put it, "To my grandfather, the Sabbath was the Lord's holy day; to my father, it was the Sabbath; to me, it's the weekend." We've lost a sense of the sacredness of time.

DAVID: Is it possible to win back the ground that we've lost?

BEN: Yes. God commands nothing that is not possible. I think we *must* win back the ground.

DAVID: Is keeping the Sabbath a suggestion from God, or does he have stronger feelings than that?

BEN: It's one of the Ten *Commandments*. What can I say? I know many Christians who scrupulously obey nine out of the ten, but are cavalier about this one. People who wouldn't dream of committing adultery or lying or stealing or blaspheming God's holy name will regularly violate the Sabbath.

DAVID: Can we push this restoration of the Sabbath so much that we enter into a new type of legalism?

BEN: I'm sure we could do that. We're sinners, we'll always manage to mess something up. But I don't think we need to worry about legalism today. That's the last thing I worry about as I look at the people in my congregation. I have the feeling that, Sunday after Sunday, the people sitting in the pews are always on their way someplace else. The day is already full up, and the earlier the service, the better, so they can get on and do whatever it is they wanted to do the rest of the day.

DAVID: Aren't people tempted to do some normal work on their day of rest like they would the rest of the week?

BEN: Certainly. Often I have walked into my room, seen the pile of stuff lying on my desk, and heard it calling to me. So I say, out loud, "Nope. I don't belong to you. I belong to the Lord, and I'm not going to do this today."

DAVID: Great! What does man lose when he violates God's principle of the Sabbath?

BEN: First of all, he loses grace. All the graciousness of life starts draining out when all I have to do is work. There's no stopping. When my whole life is defined by deadlines and the work I feel I must do, it is wonderful to be able to stop and to say, "I live by grace, not by works."

He also loses freedom. In the Deuteronomy 5 list of the Ten Commandments, the theological rationale for the Sabbath is to remember that once you were slaves and now you are free. I go back to that pile of stuff on my desk and say, "I don't belong to you; I'm a free man. I belong to God." God warned Israel to observe the Sabbath lest they forget they were free. There's great freedom in stopping, regardless of what's yelling at you to get it done.

DAVID: What about you personally? What are you doing to avoid being unbalanced regarding work and worship?

BEN: Loretta, my wife, and I have two rules. One is that we begin our Sabbath (my day off, which is not Sunday) the evening before my day off. That's a very important rule. If I have to have a meeting, I would rather have it on the evening of my day off than the evening before my day off. There's a qualitative difference in how I feel and the rest I get if I begin my day off the evening before. If Sunday were my day off, I'd begin Sabbath observance on Saturday evening to get ready for church on Sunday.

DAVID: Sounds revolutionary! What about rule number two?

BEN: We put it as a little aphorism: "If it's 'necessary,' don't do it." I put "necessary" in quotation marks because there are some things that simply must be done. But there's a host of things that feel necessary which really aren't. When Loretta and I feel the "necessity" of those things, we lay down, take an aspirin, and wait until the feeling goes away.

DAVID: How would you translate that to those whose day of rest is Sunday?

BEN: I would tell them, first of all, to see the day as belonging to God, not to them. Second, to realize that he has given them this day for their sake, and that they should pursue and enjoy and appreciate the things on that day which enhance their sense of rest and the goodness of God. There's wide latitude for Christians to observe the Sabbath.

End-of-the-Day Replay

1. Remove distractions

2. Rerun the events of your day

3. Respond to Christ's evaluation

I sensed Christ said to me:

"This was well done: _____

_____

_____."

"Work harder on this: _____

_____

_____."

☐ I have established a support relationship with another Christian and am meeting at least once a week.

Rest, Then Work, II

Friday, Day Thirty-Four

Christ wants to transform my daily work. Through today's Scripture, Nehemiah 13:15-22, he is saying to me specifically, "_____, *in your work situation* _____ _____. "

DAVID: Work and worship are two primary words in relationship to our lives. Ben, how close are the two biblical words for work and worship?

BEN: The words are almost indistinguishable. The same word that refers to service in the sanctuary can also refer to service in the world. Both in Hebrew and Greek, you have to look at the context in which the word appears in order to determine which one it's referring to. Service done to God in the world or service done to God in the sanctuary are the same word.

DAVID: How are your people doing in this regard? Are they able to look at work and worship as the same, offered to God?

BEN: They're trying hard. In many ways it's a matter of unlearning years of conditioning. My church is filled with people who have, at least on the surface, highly satisfying jobs—well

173

paying, highly responsible, pretty high profile—but by their own admission they've been at a loss to connect their work with their faith. They're in two categories: "work" and "whatever else I do for God."

DAVID: You write about the liturgy of work. What are we supposed to understand by that term?

BEN: All of life is service rendered to God. All work that's worth doing is work that God wants done. That's a tough standard, by the way. If we asked some hard questions, we might find we wouldn't do some of the work we're doing. I'm not saying which jobs—obviously, you couldn't be a hit man for the mafia. But there are many other jobs which might be hard to justify before God.

But there's another dimension to this beside doing things that God wants done. It's that in the doing of these things we experience a fellowship with God. Paul says, "Do everything as to the Lord." I think of the slaves that Paul was addressing, men and women who probably were doing meaningless work. But Paul said, "You can still do this as an offering to God." I believe we can work as did Brother Lawrence, the Benedictine monk who washed dishes and was in continuous fellowship with Jesus Christ. Or like the poet George Herbert who said, "Teach me, my God and king, in all things thee to see in what I do. In anything, to do it as unto thee." Work can be a fellowship with God, a communion, an offering to him.

DAVID: You talk about work and worship being "sacramental." What do you mean?

BEN: By sacramental, I mean with a small "s." It's interesting that the Latin word from which we get our word sacramental is the word *sacramentum*. A *sacramentum* was a pledge of absolute loyalty that a Roman soldier made to his commanding officers. When the church used this word *sacramentum* to apply to the Lord's supper and to baptism, it was saying that God is pledging himself to us. When I talk about sacraments with a small "s," I'm saying that in all of life, we meet God. He mediates his presence to us. He shows us his love and his care and his concern. Work can be a sacramental activity if done as unto him, because it's in the work we can meet God and have fellowship with him.

DAVID: If we were to ask, "What's the opposite of work?" many people would reply, "Play." You're saying the opposite is not play, but rest. Could you define that?

BEN: Paradoxically, it's the opposite of work that makes work healthy and worthwhile. It's stopping our work, to rest and to worship, that makes work a possibility for fulfillment.

DAVID: I always wonder when someone writes a book if the author feels passionately about the subject, or writes simply because it's interesting. How would you respond to that?

BEN: I feel passionately that if God is God, and he made this wonderful world, that we ought to be able to walk in fellowship with him in every area of life, especially if we know Jesus Christ. Think of it! A typical person in my congregation might work fifty to sixty hours a week. What a tragedy it would be to spend fifty or sixty hours a week—most of your waking hours—out of fellowship with God, not in communion with him.

DAVID: Is there a way that worship on Sunday prepares us to work "sacramentally" on Monday and through the rest of the week?

BEN: Absolutely. In worship we gain the vision of life that informs everything else we do out in the world.

DAVID: Do you feel that there's a need for a realignment on Sunday so people will learn how to get things set up straight?

BEN: There will be no fellowship with God in work Monday through Friday unless we learn how to fellowship with God on Sunday. If God can't be real to us at the Lord's table, then he won't be real to us at our desk or at the workbench.

DAVID: In some ways, when we use the word *worship* or *rest*, people think of what goes on in the church on Sunday morning. Are you using those terms in a broader context so that it involves other parts of Sunday as well?

BEN: Absolutely. Part of the day is spent in the sanctuary with God's people. But the rest of the day is a time to savor all the things that make life worthwhile. Certainly it's our Lord and Savior Jesus Christ. It's his salvation. But it's also our family, it's the goodness of his creation. In order to savor anything you need to slow down and not gulp it in, but rather taste it and savor it.

And let me say something about recreation here. I don't believe there's any particular recreation that absolutely should not be done on the Sabbath. But there's a frenetic drivenness about recreation in our culture. People go out and just play their heads

175

off, "recreating." In that sense, they approach play with the same intensity and drivenness that they take to work. What I'd like them to learn is to re-create in a spiritual way, to balance worship and work, or rest and work. Only in that way will they ever find wholeness in life.

End-of-the-Day Replay

1. Remove distractions

2. Rerun the events of your day

3. Respond to Christ's evaluation

I sensed Christ said to me:

"This was well done: _____

_____

_____."

"Work harder on this: _____

_____

_____."

☐ This week I gave away three presents of Christ and recorded this information on page 152.

Three Ways to Restore

Saturday, Day Thirty-Five

Christ wants to transform my daily work. Through today's Scripture, Luke 6:1-11, he is saying to me specifically,
"_____, *in your work situation*
_____
_____."

STEVE: When I think of a hard worker, I can't help but think of "Little Gram," Nellie Braniff. I call her Little Gram because that's what our kids call her. She's ninety-six years old, and right now is just about the same size as our twelve-year-old son Brendan.

VALERIE: Little Gram is my mother's mom, my grandmother. I remember her always chock-full of energy. We call her a tornado in reverse because wherever she goes, order and cleanliness follow. I especially remember her for two things. First, as she was cleaning, she would sing. She really enjoyed it. Second was her spouting pithy statements, things like, "Cleanliness is next to godliness." I particularly remember one statement I never understood as a child. When she got discouraged with having to clean up after us yet again that day, she would say, "There's no rest for the wicked." I always wondered what she meant; I knew she wasn't wicked. But I knew she needed rest. I've since thought about that, and I believe a lot of people feel that way. They wonder what they did wrong in their childhood that they have to work so hard now.

STEVE: Many people sense their work is a result of the curse. But Scripture declares there was work before the curse. God placed Adam in the garden to work or to tend the garden. Then he gave him Eve to be a suitable helpmeet. It was only after the curse that thorns came and work got much harder, even painful. It was then that they had to earn their living by the sweat of their brow.

Interestingly, in Ecclesiastes 3, we are told that work is a gift of God, that we should find satisfaction in what we do. While God has given us work, he recognizes we have a tendency to overwork, to continue to producing. He doesn't want that.

VALERIE: Some of us are consumed with what we do. We're not happy until every thorn is gone, every thistle pulled. I also believe God knew that as long as there were strong and weak people, the strong would have a tendency to oppress the weak with work. We see this both in the Bible and in history. Even children have not been able to escape the oppressors in work.

STEVE: There are places around the world where that is still true, where people are taken advantage of, overworked, oppressed. God doesn't want us always to produce. That's why he built, in his good design, a rhythm of six days for work and one day for rest. We need that one day to restore and to refocus. Life is more than work. Man is not merely an animal. We are not machines.

VALERIE: Life is to be relationships. Machines don't have relationships. I like to picture Adam and Eve after they get their work done, taking a step back, holding hands, and saying, "Isn't that beautiful? Isn't that gorgeous?" They took time to smell the roses.

STEVE: Life is also spiritual. You need time to build communion with God. There may be a lot of pressing demands on your schedule. Maybe when you come home from the end of a day's work there aren't that many free hours for you to do something else. But it's important to take time to restore. If we don't, we will become chronically tired, increasingly worn out, and eventually won't be as productive as we'd like.

VALERIE: God is an amazingly good planner, and this Sabbath plan comes out of his heart of love for us. But sometimes we don't take advantage of his design. We work all seven days and forget the Sabbath was set aside for us to gain balance and perspective. When we forget it, we only cheat ourselves.

STEVE: It's important to make time for restoration—to be renewed, to give attention to the soul. We need to feed our souls and do something positive, not just do something that occupies time and distracts us from the pressures of the week.

VALERIE: Many of us fall into the trap of merely relieving our boredom. We plop ourselves in front of the TV and wonder why we go back to work on Monday feeling like we don't want to face it again. It's because that time in front of the TV didn't do anything. It didn't satisfy us, it didn't feed our soul. It just spent hours anesthetizing us. We need to find something that will make us say, "I am ready now to go back and do this work with renewed vigor. I am recharged, ready to attack what's before me."

STEVE: We have three specific suggestions on how to restore ourselves. The first two apply to everyone, the third you'll have to personalize.

VALERIE: First, we need to spend time with the Lord alone, to come to him and talk freely and openly and honestly. We need to spend time listening for his voice through his word and through the quietness of our hearts as his Spirit speaks to us. I have undergone times of great despondency, discouragement, even anger. But when I came to the Lord and spent some time with him, before long I was turned 180 degrees around. Maybe it meant I had to repent of some sin in my life. Maybe it was that suddenly I had a new perspective. Whatever it was, he restored me in that time and sent me out a new person.

STEVE: Second, we need time to build relationships with our friends and family. One of the beautiful things about the church is that it provides both of these first two specifics. It is there that we find time to be with God for worship with others of like mind, and also time to be involved in relationships with people who care about us and love us.

VALERIE: Third, we need "time to smell the roses." Time to recreate, or re-create ourselves. It's finding that meaningful activity that will boost us, that will do more than just fill the time—something that will give us a sense of satisfaction, a sense of completion, a sense of worth.

STEVE: Some people find this in a hobby. I find it refreshing and restorative to work with my hands, to work with a piece of wood or do some project that can be completed. In ministry, you don't always see instant results. I like it when I can do something and say, "That's done; I never have to do that again."

VALERIE: I enjoy getting a good book, putting on some beautiful music, going to bed early, and reading until I fall asleep. That's my idea of regenerating, of getting my batteries recharged.

STEVE: To take advantage of the Lord's good design, we must seek ways to restore ourselves. Spend time evaluating how you're doing in these three key areas of rest. First, the spiritual: Are you spending time restoring your soul? Second, the social: Are you spending time building relationships? Third, the physical: Are you spending time smelling the roses? It's all-important if you want to enjoy this wonderful world that God has given us.

S.B., V.B.

End-of-the-Day Replay

1. Remove distractions

2. Rerun the events of your day

3. Respond to Christ's evaluation

I sensed Christ said to me:

"This was well done: _____

_____

_____."

"Work harder on this: _____

_____

_____."

☐ I remembered to pray the Ultimate Authority Prayer today.

Week Five Notes

1. Garth Lean, *Strangely Warmed* (Wheaton, Ill.: Tyndale House, 1979), p. 65.

2. Leonard Ravenhill, *Revival God's Way* (Minneapolis: Bethany House, 1983), pp. 102-104.

Learn the Balance of Work and Rest

Even God rested after six days of hard work.
We need to take time out, too,
not only to meet with other believers on Sunday,
but also to let God refresh our bodies and spirits.

Week Six:
Recording Progress

Bridge the Gap between Church and Work
(Details on page 13.)

To help bridge the church/work gap I completed assignment number _____ on _____(date). The experience taught me that _____

_____

_____

_____.

Delight Others by Giving Away the Presents of Christ
(Details on page 18.)

This week I tried to delight others by giving the presents of Christ three times in the following ways:

1. On _____ I gave a present of _____

    to _____.

2. On _____ I gave a present of _____

    to _____.

3. On _____ I gave a present of _____

    to _____.

Keeping Balanced
Sunday, Day Thirty-Six

Christ wants to transform my daily work. Through today's Scripture, Mark 6:30-46, he is saying to me specifically,
"_____, *in your work situation*
_____
_____."

═══

If someone accuses you of being unbalanced, it's unlikely he or she is paying you a compliment.

Most of us prize balance. To lose our balance is embarrassing. To get out of balance is to risk being seen as unstable . . . and "unstable" is a terrible word to appear on a letter of recommendation for college or a job.

Balance . . . would you believe it's even hard to keep balanced spiritually?

In the Scriptures we learn that from the beginning God established a balance between work and rest. Men worked during the day and rested in the evening. All of us know the wonderful restorative value of sleep. We go to bed exhausted both physically and mentally, but with a good night's rest we can wake up refreshed, creative, and productive. We don't have to sleep as much as we're awake, but without a proper ratio the lack of balance catches up with us.

That is why the Lord established the weekly Sabbath:

So on the seventh day he rested from all his work. And God blessed the seventh day and made it holy . . . (Genesis 2:2-3).

As with the need for daily physical rest, the Sabbath was a time for restoring spiritually. On this one day out of seven, man was more than a worker. On the Sabbath he could concentrate on the dignity that was his as God's child.

Are you beginning to see that God views rest as more than just ceasing from work? It's more than taking a nap, more than a mere change of pace, more than faithfully attending church. It's being reminded that we truly are children of God.

Jesus is a good model for us to follow. Jesus worked hard like most of us do, yet could never seem to catch up on all the demands placed on him. But Jesus also knew when he was spiritually drained and when he needed to break from the demands—and *rest*.

Have you come to that place? Do you sometimes say, "I need time for the real world of the spiritual so I can better cope with the secular unreality surrounding me"? Jesus intuitively knew the proper ratio between work and rest. For him it was more than a code to go by. What about us?

I believe God wants us to learn this special awareness from his Son. The balance for you may be different than the balance for me. But all people benefit when God's children learn the balance between work and rest.

We can't expect the world to know this balance. Natural men don't understand the things of the Spirit. Consider the crowds described in Mark 6:30-46 when Jesus fed the five thousand. They little appreciated that Christ and his twelve needed time to recharge in God's presence. What did they know about feedings of this kind? Their stomachs enjoyed a good fish sandwich, but their spirits didn't know about another kind of feeding. How good it is that Christ knew what was best—not only for him, but in the long run for the crowd as well! We must learn from Christ.

The world needs what we alone have. A story might make my point clear.

In the early 1900s a shepherd named Elzeard Bouffier tended his flock high in the Alps near Provence, France. The area was a barren and colorless land where nothing grew but wild lavender. Former villages lay desolate, springs had run dry, and the wind blew with unendurable ferocity.

One day a mountain climber named Jean Giono came upon Bouffier's small hut while searching for water. He was invited in to share a meal and to rest for the evening. After dinner, Giono's host dumped a small sack of acorns on the table and began to meticulously search for precisely one hundred perfect specimens—without cracks, without damage, without imperfections of any kind. The next morning the shepherd planted these specially selected nuts.

In three years Bouffier had planted 100,000 acorns, of which twenty thousand had sprouted. Half of those were expected to die, leaving ten thousand oak trees to grow where nothing had grown before.

Giono then lost track of Bouffier until after the First World War. When he did visit, he discovered an avalanche of living color. Green hillsides replaced barrenness, brooks once again flowed with clear water. Willows, rushes, meadows, gardens, and flowers had reappeared. Villages had been repopulated.

Then came World War II, and another visit was postponed until hostilities ceased. But what a sight greeted Giono upon his return! Less than twenty miles from the lines, Bouffier had peacefully continued his work, ignoring the war of 1939 as he had ignored that of 1914. "On the site of the ruins I had seen in 1913 now stand neat farms," Giono wrote. "The old streams, fed by the rains and snows that the forest conserves, are flowing again. . . . Little by little the villages have been rebuilt. People from the plains, where land is costly, have settled here bringing youth, motion, the spirit of adventure. Along the roads you meet hearty men and women, boys and girls who understand laughter and have recovered a taste for picnics. Counting the former population, unrecognizable now that they live in comfort, more than ten thousand people owe their happiness to Elzeard Bouffier."[1]

All because of a simple shepherd who dedicated himself to reclaiming a barren world. All because one simple man knew the importance of his work. He knew that people needed the shade his trees would provide. He knew men and women needed the strength those oaks embodied, the roots that anchored fertile soil to the earth, the vision of grandeur they supplied.

Do you see the spiritual lesson here? Our society hungers for the forests, the leafy sanctuaries, the shaded paths. Harvey Cox, in his book *Turning East*, says Westerners are flocking to Eastern meditation because, "It provides a modern equivalent of what the observance of Sabbath once did but does no more." But why turn to Eastern meditation? We already know what we need. We need a renewal of holiness, a replanting of things sacred, and at the head of the list must be a rediscovery of the Sabbath.

All people benefit when God's children learn the balance between work and rest. And what might God be saying to *you*?

D.M., K.M.

End-of-the-Day Replay

1. Remove distractions

2. Rerun the events of your day

3. Respond to Christ's evaluation

I sensed Christ said to me:

"This was well done: _____

_____

_____."

"Work harder on this: _____

_____

_____."

☐ To bridge the church/work gap I have completed one of the weekly assignments and recorded this information on page 184.

Follow the Directions

Monday, Day Thirty-Seven

Christ wants to transform my daily work. Through today's Scripture, Isaiah 40:27-31, he is saying to me specifically, "_____, in your work situation

_____

_____."

You've probably heard about the man who wanted his money back for the box of mothballs he bought. He said they didn't work. He'd tried the entire box, and couldn't hit a single moth!

He should have read the directions, right?

The Mains family, always on the go, recently decided it needed to learn to relax more. So we bought a family game and set aside an evening to play it. My son Randall and my new daughter-in-law Carmel came over to join us.

"The Garden Game" is a prizewinner, but it's also complicated, with four pages of directions. Once we got into it, we really enjoyed it. We laughed a lot but no one seemed able to win. Finally, Jeremy, my youngest, challenged Randall on something he did. "Back off, Jeremy, that's fair!" responded Randy. He got out the directions and re-read them. "Golly! If I'd known that," moaned Jeremy, "I could have won a half-hour ago. Look!" Sure enough, he had not only everything he needed to win, but also everything anybody else needed to win. Shades of the mothball story!

When it comes to directions regarding daily work, God gives us some guidelines. I was surprised by how many Bible passages speak on this topic. It's one of those areas where God lays out clear instructions about balancing work with rest. The fourth commandment reads, "Remember the Sabbath day by keeping it holy. Six days you shall labor and do all your work, but the seventh day is a Sabbath to the LORD your God."

The Hebrew word for sabbath, *shabbat*, means "to cease from doing," or to rest. Now, I know we don't become Christians by following the Ten Commandments, but even so, they remain a valid code of conduct—simple directions given by a loving Creator as to how his creatures should live. As I list the commandments, see if you think one or two of them should be dropped:

1. Don't lie.

2. Don't steal.

3. Don't commit adultery.

4. Don't murder.

5. Don't take God's name in vain.

6. Don't have other gods.

7. Don't covet what someone else has.

8. Don't make idols.

9. Honor your parents.

10. Keep the Sabbath.

What do you think? I believe a loving God gave these instructions for our benefit so we could function at peak performance. I don't believe the Lord imposed these on us to restrict us in some way. These commandments are for our good as individuals and also for society. And because more space is given to the sabbath commandment than any other, it appears this principle of balancing work with rest is quite important.

You know what that means, don't you? If American Christians are to follow God's directions regarding the Sabbath, it's going to take some major adjustments.

Let me speak personally. Years ago my family confronted me on my problem with "workaholism." I may have thought other problems were more pressing, but they all made it clear this was the one I needed to come to grips with. It had caused them real pain.

I remember confessing on a broadcast that I was attacking my problem. One sympathetic listener wrote and said I was brave to admit on the air that I was "alcoholic." My, what a difference a couple of letters make! The two problems do have something in common: Beating my workaholism has been as hard for me as it is for others to beat alcoholism.

But I'm improving. The Lord is really helping me; my wife especially will testify to that. That's why I could play a family game the other night. I made adjustments in the following three areas regarding rest:

First, rest from work involves restoring spiritually. In this regard, I'm making big changes in my Sunday observance. I've not become a legalist; I've carefully avoided that. But I'm aware that our culture had affected me more than I would admit.

Second, I'm improving in the relational area. I'm learning not to be consumed by work. As a full human being, I am to value human relationships even as I do my relationship with the Lord. To shut the briefcase even though there's another broadcast to be written has been good for me. At certain times it's more important to spend time with my wife or my children or my parents or my brother and sister-in-law or with good friends.

The third area is something I'm still working on. I have a way to go in terms of "smelling the roses." I'm still searching for a good way to re-create, to find something I really enjoy that's not work-related—something about which I can say, "This is fun for me. I enjoy this." That's my next project.

It's for our own good to learn the balance of work and rest. If we want to function at top performance it's important to follow the directions God lays out. Otherwise, *we* are like the guy who says, "These mothballs are no good! I couldn't hit a single moth with them!" Everyone laughs because they all know he's stupid for doing it all wrong.

Too often, man thinks he knows what's best. But by going against God's work/rest guidelines, he always loses. Maybe he loses his marriage or family. Maybe he loses his health or his spiritual edge or his testimony. But he always loses when he ignores what God has said.

So follow the directions. *His* directions. Do it so you can function at top performance. If changes need to be made in your life in order to balance work with rest, begin with what God already has said.

I believe that some people, like my son Jeremy, are going to find they already have in hand what they need in order to win.

D.M.

End-of-the-Day Replay

1. Remove distractions

2. Rerun the events of your day

3. Respond to Christ's evaluation

I sensed Christ said to me:

"This was well done: _____

_____

_____."

"Work harder on this: _____

_____

_____."

☐ I am remembering this week to give away three of the presents of Christ and to record this information on page 184.

Get Some Rest

Tuesday, Day Thirty-Eight

Christ wants to transform my daily work. Through today's Scripture, 1 Timothy 6:6-10, he is saying to me specifically, "_____, *in your work situation*

_____

_____."

Did you sleep well last night? I didn't. Because of an emergency, I slept only a couple of hours.

Most adults sleep from seven to eight and one-half hours each night. Some can get by with an average of six. But deprived of sleep for even two days, concentration becomes difficult. Tasks can be performed for short periods, but mistakes multiply and the person grows irritable and easily distracted.

Persons who go without sleep for three days have great difficulty thinking clearly, hearing clearly, and seeing clearly. They lose track of their thoughts in the middle of a sentence. Soon, hallucinations begin.

We need our rest. If we choose to, we can ignore these warning signs, but God has made us in such a way that before long a lack of proper rest catches up with us.

Don't misunderstand. Work is a privilege. I'm leery of people who don't work. Rear a son or daughter who doesn't know how to

193

work and you've done that child a disservice.

But teach him or her about rest as well. There is a time to earn your keep but there's also a time to be a family, to enjoy the company of friends, to nurture the soul by drawing close to God himself.

When is such rest needed? When all the work is done? No. Often, the work is never done. God knew this so from the beginning he established the Sabbath principle of one day of rest in every seven. As man must have physical rest each night, so each week he must have rest for his spirit.

Jesus knew when it was time to rest. He worked hard, very hard, but there were always more people to heal than he could get to. There were always latecomers who missed his sermons. Always those who said, "I didn't get to see the last miracle. Do another one, please." Always more reports to hear from disciples training to carry on his work.

Listen to Mark 6:30-31: "The apostles gathered around Jesus and reported to him all they had done and taught. Then, because so many people were coming and going that they did not even have a chance to eat, he said to them, 'Come with me by yourselves to a quiet place and get some rest.' "

As a young man in his early thirties, Jesus knew what it took me until my late forties to find out: Rest is determined by how much you've done, not by how much remains to be done.

On the surface, that doesn't sound too revolutionary. But for me, it was life-transforming. I would work all day, stay at the office until everyone was gone, start the next morning at my desk very early, travel and preach on the weekends, and be at it again in the studio early Monday morning. There was always more to do—partly because I kept taking on more. I couldn't say no.

In those years I had a lot of strength. What I didn't understand was that even Jesus, the Son of God, couldn't meet every need—not when limited to the frailties of a human body like us.

One healing resulted in many other pitiful people with infirmities also coming for help. Lines and lines of them.

One conversation with Zaccheus only opened up countless other Zaccheus-types who wanted him to come by for dinner and conversation.

That's why in the Gospels we find Jesus sleeping on a storm-tossed boat when everyone else is struggling to keep it afloat. He doesn't get up and say, "Hey, oh, please forgive me for not helping. I'm sorry, I'm sorry!" No. He had given out much more than any of them, and he knew he deserved some rest.

Would another hand at the oars have been helpful? Probably. But for Christ, what had been done was more important than what still needed to be done.

Only when I first began to think this way did my sin of workaholism begin to be mastered. I purposely said "sin" because not only did it violate some of God's commands, but it was hurting the people I loved the most.

Karen was so helpful. "Don't tell me what has to be done," she'd say when I finally got home. "Tell me what you did."

"Well, I finished a program. I dictated about a dozen letters. I met with the staff. I got tomorrow's program worked out. I had prayer with a couple who was hurting. Let's see—and I wrote the lead article for the newsletter."

"No wonder you're so tired," she would say. "How did you do it? Could any other man have done all those things in one day and as well as you did them, David?"

"Probably not," I'd say, really meaning it in my heart, still tired.

"Well, I think you deserve to rest now," she'd respond.

"But look what's left to do!"

"No, don't," she'd caution. "Just look at what you've done. That's how you know when it's time to stop for awhile and recuperate. Now, tell me again all you did today."

So I'd go back through the list. Sometimes it wore me out just listing everything!

When you've given out a lot, there needs to be time to take in, to re-create, to rest. It probably doesn't matter what has yet to be done. Some of us could work a lifetime and never get it done.

I'm learning. And I'm glad! My call for revival has to be more than just a challenge to spiritual workaholism. Like some of you, I know of districts in our country that have been revivaled-out in past years. That concerns me. Somebody pushed too hard.

Revival expectations should never violate God's emphasis on the importance of rest and the maintenance of daily work. So work hard . . . and rest deeply. And let's believe that through these adventure disciplines, God can begin to transform our daily work.

D.M.

End-of-the-Day Replay

1. Remove distractions

2. Rerun the events of your day

3. Respond to Christ's evaluation

I sensed Christ said to me:

"This was well done: _____

_____

_____."

"Work harder on this: _____

_____

_____."

☐ I remembered to pray the Ultimate Authority Prayer today.

Playaholics and Workaholics[2]

Wednesday, Day Thirty-Nine

Christ wants to transform my daily work. Through today's Scripture, Proverbs 3:9, 10, he is saying to me specifically,

"_____, *in your work situation*

_____

_____."

When an intense young man with workaholic inclinations marries a free-spirited young woman who equates work with "to be coerced," there's bound to be a clash.

His dedication takes a briefcase even to extended family gatherings—picnics, for instance. Her native woman-of-leisure mentality pictures literary discussions at breakfast . . . with someone else to wash the dishes; lunch with a friend after viewing the latest art institute exhibit . . . while a nanny watches the children; an evening set aside for reading . . . with a cook to prepare dinner.

Can a workaholic marry a playaholic? Yes! I know it's possible, because it happened—*to me!* And you can only imagine the tensions involved.

I hate anything which causes me to sweat. For David, work is play. But take heart! Our marital tension between work and play is being resolved by understanding the spiritual principle of re-creation.

To some Christians, work represents the *summum bonum*—man's highest good. They feel guilty if they take time out for themselves, if they spend money on vacation, or if they're caught napping. Often, these folks are the backbone of a pastor's stable of volunteer lay workers.

For other Christians, work is only a financial means to an end: ski excursions, fishing trips, or membership in a racquetball club. These are the folks who endure their jobs but can hardly wait for leisurely weekends or evenings of television. A pastor-friend in a temperate climate put it this way: "It's hard to get people to work. Everyone seems to be out on the tennis court."

Too many of us unconsciously live either for work or for pleasure—a form of idolatry either way. And the pursuit of either, as an end in itself, is fruitless.

God, in love, gives us rest. And because he well knows the wandering heart of his creation, he made it into law. Erich Fromm, the Jewish writer, states: "Rest in the sense of the traditional Sabbath concept is quite different from rest being defined as not working or not making an effort. On the Sabbath, man ceases completely to fight for survival and to sustain his biological life. On the Sabbath, man is fully man, with no task other than to be human."[3]

The purpose of Sabbath rest is physical and emotional renewal, but it's also fellowship—a delightful space in the weekly calendar reserved for becoming better acquainted with ourselves, with others, and with God. It's a time for a good talk, for laughter, for thinking about serious ideas, and for sharing intimacies between Creator and creature. Our souls are replenished, quieted, nurtured, caressed.

Rest without spiritual rest is incomplete. We cannot find true renewal when we deny the spiritual. That helps explain the frantic search for leisure activities in our culture, this rushing off to one weekend event after another, then breathlessly returning when Sunday is ended.

The Sabbath principle, properly understood, is rest from the bondage of work. God is concerned about our freedom. Psalm 127:2 declares, "It is senseless for you to work so hard from early morning until late at night, fearing you will starve to death; for God wants his loved ones to get their proper rest" (TLB).

Rest is different for all people. I renew by reading, taking walks, listening to music, gardening, having a small group of people in our home, good talks, writing in my journal, and by prayer. David rests by having time to strategize a future project, driving in the car and thinking, watching Shakespeare, roughhousing with the boys, and working in his prayer journal.

I often slip into cycles of not sleeping well at night. An early riser, I'm fatigued by 9 P.M., so I go to bed early and sleep lightly. Noises—like dogs barking, children returning home, conversations in the hallway—can easily rouse me, so I'm often awake for several hours. These periods often occur when my mind is overloaded with projects. Somehow, I just can't seem to wind down.

How wonderful it is in the middle of one of these cycles to sleep, to sleep deeply, to awake rested and truly renewed. "Oh, I slept well last night!" I announce to my husband, whose sleepless nights within the last year can be counted on one hand.

Sabbath rest is like a good sleep after insomnia. It brings respite to man's cruel struggle for existence. It speaks "shalom," peace, to our restless souls.

So how has this understanding helped the workaholic in our family? And how has it helped the playaholic? It's doing wonders!

For David, observing Sunday has meant learning to recreate. He's learning not to take on more work than he can do in a week. He's learning to put it aside and take authority over its control in his life. He's learning to relax, to play, to enjoy something other than the grindstone.

When we keep Sunday with Sabbath understanding, a resurrection process goes on in each of us. When we cease from our work, and let Christ do his work within us, we realize that our work is not so important. We can stop, and the world goes on! It's God's activity, not ours, that is important.

Conversely, we must joyfully participate in Sunday without the nagging reminder of unmet deadlines and unfinished housework. For the playaholic, I know I have six days in which to complete as much as can be completed. And then I can truly put aside the weight of responsibilities. By starting early in the week to anticipate Sunday, I find that I am better organized in my housework, in my writing, and in my broadcasting schedule—all with the wonderful reward that on Saturday, while getting ready for Sunday, I will begin to rest, to rest deeply, and simply begin to *be*.

Well, I know a workaholic who once upon a time married a playaholic. David Mains married Karen Burton. Is there help for this marriage? Yes. An understanding of the sacred rhythm of work and play puts life into proper perspective.

Six days shall you work, but on the seventh you shall refrain from working. "[It] is a sabbath to the LORD your God."

That's the principle that's healing this split in my marriage. Could it help you?

K.M.

End-of-the-Day Replay

1. Remove distractions

2. Rerun the events of your day

3. Respond to Christ's evaluation

I sensed Christ said to me:

"This was well done: _____

_____

_____."

"Work harder on this: _____

_____

_____."

☐ I have given away at least one of the presents of Christ this week and have recorded this information on page 184.

He's a Fisherman, not a Hunter

Thursday, Day Forty

Christ wants to transform my daily work. Through today's Scripture, Matthew 9:35-38, he is saying to me specifically,
"_____, *in your work situation*

_____

_____. "

━━━━━
━━━━━

DAVID: Rebecca Manley Pippert, your book on evangelism, *Out of the Saltshaker and Into the World,* has been popular for many years now. I think part of its popularity is that you share your fears and failures; readers quickly identify with your fumblings and bumblings. Should mistakes be expected in witnessing?

BECKY: Yes, because we continue to be human beings when Christ comes into our lives. Making a mistake in evangelism can be redeemed, it can be used. Scripture says, "I will be glorified in your weakness." Our difficulty is that we want God to be glorified only in our strength. We think, *Unless I can do it perfectly, I won't say anything.* But God can use even our mistakes.

I have often failed. I've blown it, I've said something insensitive and have agonized over it. Then I thought, *Why am I agonizing alone?* So I went back to that person and said, "I blew it, and I'm so

201

sorry. As I thought about it, I would like to say this. . . ." For some reason, we think once we've said something, it can never be erased—we can't ever change anything. But that isn't true.

DAVID: You write that one of your early mistakes was to think that you had to give the whole ball of wax at one time. Would doing something kind at an office or factory be witnessing?

BECKY: It certainly is. Witnessing involves both word and deed. But I think the deed is frankly more important, because if I am witnessing with my words and don't have a life to back it up, it can be detrimental. Whether we like it or not, the first Bible most people read is our life.

DAVID: You also talk about discussing with another Christian how you're doing in sharing your faith. We Christians don't discuss enough with each other how to touch others with the beauty of Christ, do we?

BECKY: I don't think so. We're talking about being brothers and sisters to one another. It's critical for my spiritual growth to have people who understand me, know me, share my burdens and my pain. If I say, "I think I blew it," they can say, "Yes, that's right."

DAVID: You also say witnessing doesn't have to be so much telling God's truth as it is asking good questions. I'm curious about that.

BECKY: God is a tremendous storyteller, and he always asks questions. But what do we do? Too often, we give answers and preach sermons. We should begin with the model of Scripture—learn to be a storyteller and also how to ask good questions.

DAVID: What would be a good question?

BECKY: It depends on the level of your relationship. If I'm at the point of investigating and don't know the person well, I want to know about his experience with the church, about how her views of God have changed, etc. If I'm not merely investigating but trying to arouse curiosity in the gospel, then I'll say something like, "Just curious—what was your analysis, having read the New Testament documents? What did you think?"

DAVID: What if someone responds, "I thought it was crazy!"

BECKY: I'd say, "And when did you come to that conclusion?" More often than not it was when he or she was in Sunday school. I rarely find any adult who's examined the New Testament documents with an adult, critical mind. I try to help the person see the need to know what he or she is rejecting.

DAVID: So if a person says, "I can't stand church," you say, "Tell me why you feel that way."

BECKY: Absolutely. A person will say, "I cannot stand those born-again types," or will recount stories of failed Christian leaders. When most people tell me what they don't like about Christians, I agree! But I say, "Listen, that's the person's style, or the particular failure. What about the content?" They don't realize they've often thrown the baby out with the bath.

DAVID: Are you ever able to ask questions that get at the feeling level?

BECKY: The key is trying to find out where people's pain is, where they struggle. They have to know why it would make a difference to believe in God. Frankly, the evidence for the resurrection is not going to help somebody be a better mother or make a better marriage. Their circumstances and time of life will greatly determine what you talk about.

DAVID: So if a person says, "I'm lonely," you don't try to deliver the whole message of the gospel. Instead, you see if there's some way, as a Christian, you can meet that need of loneliness which opens the door for the next conversation.

BECKY: Right! Jesus has taught me that I need to tie into where people are, to try and arouse their interest in Jesus himself. If somebody is talking about loneliness or some other need, I say something like, "Jesus has a fascinating thing to say about that," and then say nothing. I wait to see if they pick up on it. Jesus often did that. When he was with the woman at the well, he said, "Of course, if you knew who was asking, you would have asked him and he would have given you living water"—and then stops speaking. He's a fisherman, not a hunter. He's reeling her in.

DAVID: When you reach out to someone on Christ's behalf, do you assume he or she is interested in what you have to say?

BECKY: If you assume the person isn't interested, you've had it. It's all over. Your whole style of communicating will be terrible. If you possibly can, assume the people you're talking to are going to be interested. If you assume they will, they probably will. If you can't pull that off, then at least don't assume the negative. Don't say to yourself, "I know this person will never be interested." That is death to a conversation. Try and find ways that God has made you alike.

One other thing I assume: People are the same. I have lived overseas, God has given me a fascinating husband, and we've been in all kinds of contexts. Wherever we've gone, we have found that people are the same. You get beneath the package and they're hurting, they want love, they want to be understood. Don't be intimidated by the package. Keep saying to yourself, "I regard no one from a human point of view anymore." See people through the eyes of Christ. They need his love.

End-of-the-Day Replay

1. Remove distractions

2. Rerun the events of your day

3. Respond to Christ's evaluation

I sensed Christ said to me:

"This was well done: _____

_____

_____."

"Work harder on this: _____

_____

_____."

☐ I have established a support relationship with another Christian and am meeting at least once a week.

He's a Fisherman, not a Hunter, II

Friday, Day Forty-One

Christ wants to transform my daily work. Through today's
Scripture, 1 Peter 3:15-16, he is saying to me specifically,
"_____, *in your work situation*

_____

_____. "

DAVID: Becky, why is it that some Christians are such good witnesses, and others seem to remain in the saltshaker?

BECKY: One answer is that evangelism is a gift; some have it, some don't. Nevertheless, my Bible doesn't say, "Go ye therefore all ye extroverts . . . all ye Scripture memory buffs . . . all ye Southern Baptists."

The main problem is that so many Christians only hang around with people like themselves. They don't have non-Christian friends. They're living with the choir. They have to get out of the saltshaker and into the world, into a relationship with people in despair and without hope.

It is critical that all of us have time for one non-Christian friend. I'll frequently hear someone say, "Well, I couldn't begin to have a ministry to non-Christians. I have too many church activities." I say, "Drop some of your church activities." I'm married to a political reporter in the secular press, and consequently there's a natural opportunity for me to meet people who do not share my faith. But even if there wasn't, I'd find it.

DAVID: How about witnessing on the job?

BECKY: That's tricky. We have to ask when the time is appropriate. I doubt your boss will be thrilled if you're using company time to begin a four-point gospel outline. It's another thing if you see an opportunity to witness that doesn't cut in on company time. Invite your co-worker out for a cup of coffee—share your faith during recess, as it were.

DAVID: Do Christians sometimes make too big a deal out of witnessing?

BECKY: Some Christians become almost paralyzed because they want to witness, they feel the intensity of the call, and then become overwhelmed and can't speak. They're almost catatonic. They need to balance a sense of urgency with a sense of time.

There's a story about three devils trying to figure out how to make Christians ineffective. One says, "Let's just tell them there's no hell, no possibility of punishment. That'll keep them quiet." The second devil disagrees: "Oh, no, let's just tell them there's no heaven, no possibility of reward." The third devil concludes, "Let's not be theologically unsound here. Let's not tell them there's no heaven or no hell; let's just tell them there's no hurry."

We need a sense of urgency, but we also must realize we're on a long journey. God will use so many different things to bring people to faith. If we feel "this is my only shot, I've got to tell them everything I know," we'll blow them out of the water. We must be sensitive to the Spirit and to this tension between urgency and patience. That leads to another issue: I am not responsible for anyone's conversion. That is not up to me. I have not failed if my contact does not become a Christian. If I am being faithful and loving, it is between God and that person. That's a monkey off my back!

DAVID: When you say "sensitive to the Holy Spirit," do you see yourself as working with the Holy Spirit?

BECKY: We are partners with God in everything we do—that's the adventure. It's so exciting to begin by praying, "OK, God, who

206

have you brought into my life? Show me. Is this the person? Is this the person?" Then I begin to sense, *This is the person God has brought to me.* So I say, "Lord, help me to be sensitive. Show me where this person is hurting. Show me his or her pain. Show me how the gospel is relevant to him or her." There is no part of the process where God and I are not talking it over.

DAVID: Sometimes we fear we'll look stupid at work if we talk to someone about the Lord or if we try to live out our faith. Is that a fair fear?

BECKY: It certainly is. There will be many times when you are asked questions you can't answer. That should never paralyze anyone. I was asked something the other day and I said, "That is a fantastic question, and I haven't a clue what the answer is. I am so glad God has brought you into my life to sharpen me intellectually." That changes things. I don't have to know everything and be everything. I'm not God; I'm Becky! I'll do the best I can.

DAVID: Do you think some Christians fear they'll offend people?

BECKY: Yes, and I think we will. The gospel itself offends some people. But just because we've offended someone doesn't mean we can't make it right. I also think we are sometimes more fearful than we need to be. One way to overcome this is to say, "I don't want to be a Bible banger. I don't want to be insensitive. If I turn you off, would you let me know?" People are amazed when they hear that. They understand we're like them.

DAVID: What about the fear that says, "If I share Christ with somebody and it doesn't work, it would be terrible"?

BECKY: I've felt that way many times! Two things have helped me overcome it. First, as you begin to walk with God you learn to rest more, and trust, and realize that evangelism is larger than us. It is God almighty at work. If this person wants to become a Christian, I am not the one who is leading him or her into salvation; it is the Holy Spirit. Second, becoming a Christian is not an emotional experience. It's an issue of the will. Whether the person "feels" something isn't the key. It's whether he or she understands the gospel, receives it as well as understands it, and recognizes that Jesus is Lord.

DAVID: You don't push a person into making a quick decision, do you? You make sure the person understands as much as possible.

BECKY: I want to be careful, though. A person doesn't have to recite the five points of Calvinism. Jesus says, "Count the cost. Reflect." At the same time, I say, "There's going to come a time when you probably will want to make a decision one way or the other. When that time comes, let me know. Is there any reason why you couldn't become a Christian?" I apply as much pressure as I dare while making sure the person understands as much as possible.

DAVID: What is the bottom line when you speak to people about evangelism?

BECKY: I hope the bottom line is freedom. I hope people will say, "God can use me in evangelism in the context of my own personality." I hope they will fall in love with Jesus and say, "In this flawed, growing person that I am, who longs to be more like God and who yet struggles, God can use even me."

End-of-the-Day Replay

1. Remove distractions

2. Rerun the events of your day

3. Respond to Christ's evaluation

I sensed Christ said to me:

"This was well done: _____

_____

_____."

"Work harder on this: _____

_____

_____."

☐ This week I gave away three presents of Christ and recorded this information on page 184.

The Difference
Jesus Has Made

Saturday, Day Forty-Two

Christ wants to transform my daily work. Through today's

Scripture, Ezekiel 20:12-20, he is saying to me specifically,

"_____, *in your work situation*

_____

_____. "

─────────
─────────
▬▬▬▬▬▬

The term *witnessing* communicates different things to different folks. To some it means passing out tracts on a street corner. To others, it's placing a clever bumper sticker on a car or writing a catchy slogan on a large rock along the highway: "Jesus saves." "Honk if you love Jesus." "Christians aren't perfect; just forgiven."

Others think witnessing is simply living a good life without saying anything about Christ. I'd call these people "Secret Service Christians."

Finally, there are believers who are thoroughly intimidated by the whole subject. Especially if witnessing is presented as a responsibility for Christians in the workplace.

There are many ways to witness. But effective witnessing in your workplace begins by establishing rapport with unbelievers.

209

This is a necessary step and it helps to remove the intimidation factor. Jesus excelled at it.

Our Lord spent most of his working days as a carpenter. The last three years of his earthly life he put aside his hammer and saw and changed vocations. He became a full-time, itinerant teacher and preacher.

In the fourth chapter of John's Gospel, Jesus models for us how to establish rapport with an unbeliever. Beginning with verse 5, we read, "[Jesus] came to a town in Samaria called Sychar. . . . Jacob's well was there, and Jesus, tired as he was from the journey, sat down by the well. . . . When a Samaritan woman came to draw water [a part of her daily work], Jesus said to her, 'Will you give me a drink?'. . . The Samaritan woman said to him, 'You are a Jew and I am a Samaritan woman. How can you ask me for a drink?' " Jews, you remember, didn't associate with Samaritans.

Note with me the approach Jesus used. From the very beginning, he related to this woman on her level. He began where she was by asking a simple question. He could have handed her a tract, or he might have grabbed her attention by quoting a few passages from the prophets condemning sin, or he could have extended her an invitation to the next series of special services at the synagogue.

But instead of intimidating her in any way, his approach sparked her interest and aroused her curiosity. Through kindness and sensitivity Jesus established rapport with her, for he, a Jew, asked a favor of a despised Samaritan woman. This was so unusual that it captured her attention. From that point on, his opportunity to witness unfolded.

The first thing you and I need to confirm in our thinking is that effective witnessing in the workplace begins by establishing rapport with unbelievers.

Chances are you already have a healthy rapport with some of your co-workers. If so, great! You're ready to go to the next step. But if not, then before today ends, try to think of some specific ways you can show interest in the life of at least one person with whom you work. I think you'll be amazed at the number of good ideas you can list in just a few minutes. Perhaps you could go out to breakfast with each other before you have to be on the job site. Or maybe you could sign up for the office bowling team for a couple of months. Or perhaps you can show some special interest in one of your co-worker's kids. It could be something as simple as asking a lot of questions of someone over a lunch break. The possibilities are almost endless.

Before inviting any unbelievers from work to a Bible study or to a meeting at your church or even before you give them a good Christian book, the best first step is to relate to them where they are. Find some common ground to establish rapport.

Let's return to John 4 and make some further observations. Jesus has taken a break from his work day. He's sitting by a well and asks a Samaritan woman a captivating question. Her curiosity is piqued. A two-way conversation ensues. Rapport continues to be established.

It's obvious that Jesus does take the initiative in directing the discussion. He looks for just the right moment to tell this person who he is. His opportunity comes in verse 25. "I know that Messiah (called Christ) is coming," the woman says. "When he comes, he will explain everything to us." "I who speak to you am he," Jesus replies.

What happens next? The woman becomes so excited, she leaves her water jar by the well, goes back to the town, and tells the others what she experienced. Her life is changed. She had met the Savior of the world.

A little later in this same passage we read, "Many of the Samaritans from that town believed in [Jesus] because of the woman's testimony."

This story highlights the need for establishing rapport with unbelievers. It also beautifully illustrates the power of personal testimony as demonstrated by this Samaritan woman.

We need to remember that after establishing rapport, witnessing is essentially telling people the difference Jesus has made in our lives. This is true in the workplace and any place. It's not enough for us merely to establish rapport with unbelievers. It's not enough to hope that those with whom we work will see Christ living through us. We dare not assume that some sort of spiritual osmosis will take place without ever talking about our faith.

Maybe your initial reaction to all of this is, "I can't do it!" Sure, you can. I'm simply suggesting that you talk about something

211

you've already experienced. What's happened to you personally? The biggest hurdle to overcome is getting started.

You may be farther down the road than you realize. If there's a sense of rapport, you'll find that most people are open to hearing what you have to say. And once you get started, mark my word, you'll be amazed at how the Spirit of God will direct your conversation step by step.

S.B.

End-of-the-Day Replay

1. Remove distractions

2. Rerun the events of your day

3. Respond to Christ's evaluation

I sensed Christ said to me:

"This was well done: _____

_____

_____."

"Work harder on this: _____

_____

_____."

☐ I remembered to pray the Ultimate Authority Prayer today.

Week Six Notes

1. Karen Mains, *Making Sunday Special* (Waco, Tex.: Word Books, 1987), pp. 141-144. Used by permission. Originally found in "The Man Who Planted Trees and Grew Happiness," by Jean Giono, published in "Friends of Nature."

2. Ibid., pp. 113-123.

3. Erich Fromm, *You Shall Be As Gods* (New York: Fawcett, 1977), p. 195.

Enjoy Introducing Jesus to Others

In our daily work, most all of us encounter people who don't know Jesus. What a pleasure to bring them into a friendship with the King!

Week Seven:
Recording Progress

Bridge the Gap between Church and Work
(Details on page 13.)

To help bridge the church/work gap I completed assignment number _____ on _____(date). The experience taught me that _____

_____

_____

_____.

━━━
━━━
━━━

Delight Others by Giving Away
the Presents of Christ
(Details on page 18.)

This week I tried to delight others by giving the presents of Christ three times in the following ways:

1. On _____ I gave a present of _____

   to _____.

2. On _____ I gave a present of _____

   to _____.

3. On _____ I gave a present of _____

   to _____.

Let the Light Out

Sunday, Day Forty-Three

Christ wants to transform my daily work. Through today's Scripture, Matthew 5:13-16, he is saying to me specifically, "_____, *in your work situation*

_____

_____ ."

Probably no topic engenders more guilt or strikes more terror in the hearts of Christian people as does sharing their faith with friends—especially where they work!

How about you? Does the subject of "witnessing" cause you to break out in a cold sweat? Well, be forewarned: That's the topic today.

So, having been prepared for the worst, let's briefly consider what our Lord had to say about witnessing in Matthew 5:13-16.

> You are the salt of the earth. But if the salt loses its saltiness, how can it be made salty again? It is no longer good for anything, except to be thrown out and trampled by men.
>
> You are the light of the world. A city on a hill cannot be hidden. Neither do people light a lamp and put it under a bowl. Instead they put it on its stand, and it gives light to everyone in the house. In the same way, let your light

shine before men, that they may see your good deeds and praise your Father in heaven.

You business managers are no doubt expecting that I have a rash of new ideas for you, such as putting a sign over your office water fountain that reads, "Everyone who drinks of this water will thirst again!" Board members may be suspecting that I'll suggest you order boxcars of gospel tracts to be peddled door-to-door like Girl Scout cookies. And college students may fear that I'm going to tell you that you must speak up for Christ the moment your science prof mentions the word *evolution*.

Now, finally, the hidden agenda of this fifty-day spiritual adventure will come to the fore!

But relax. I'm not going to lay any guilt on you. I'm not even going to suggest that you should tell others about Christ if you don't want to. I'll just say that if, more and more, you're experiencing Christ transforming your daily work, you might actually *enjoy* introducing him to others.

Unfortunately, when the word *witness* is used, people most often think of it as being verbal. But the emphasis in Matthew 5 is more on deeds than it is on words. Men and women involved in ministry full time may regularly be leading people to Christ. But almost never are they able to do this apart from someone who has lived the life before these people, which is then the reason they sought out "professional ministers" for further help. It's individuals like you who make the difference in work settings far more often than people in professional ministry.

In a job setting when jokes are continually made at another's expense, someone like you inserts Christlike words into the conversation. "That's funny," you say, "but let's be cautious in our laughter. We don't want to get Pete in a box he can't get out of. I've noticed him making an effort to correct this problem." Nothing is said about Christ. But his influence is still felt—through someone like you!

Or someone hurts on the job and you are compassionate. You show concern, and Christ is suddenly present.

Or after a convention, others claim illegitimate expenses. You only claim what you know to be fair. And the salt is there. The light shines. The city isn't hidden by clouds.

When it comes to being a witness, two extremes can be cited. One is the zealot who can talk of nothing else. He or she is pushy and at times obnoxious. That's not what I'm asking of you.

At the other extreme is the person who NEVER lets it be known that he or she belongs to the Lord. Fellow workers would be amazed to know that this person even goes to church. I don't believe you want to be that way, either!

Our great desire is to see people become part of Christ's kingdom, to see them freed from their sin, to see them come alive in Christ even as we have. But you have to start somewhere!

I don't believe the disciples were good at this at the beginning. I think they were more interested in others knowing they had an important role in something exciting. "We're part of the twelve! We're in the inner circle!" But as they matured in their relationship to the Lord, they learned to take focus off themselves and put it on Christ. That's what all of us must learn. But it takes time.

Wouldn't it be something if every time you spoke about Christ, a little voice would say to the other person, "Listen closely, you're hearing the very truth of the universe." I've learned that in a sense this is exactly what happens! The role of the Spirit is to affirm God's truth when it's spoken. The closer I come to saying what is in Scripture, the more the Spirit affirms inside the individual that what I've said is true.

I never argue with people about spiritual matters. I'm content to say, "Well, that's what the Bible says." I know that if they hear what the Bible says, the inner voice of the Spirit will sound within them. As the years have gone by, it's been interesting to hear this confirmed. "Remember when you told me that Christ could meet my need and you read that verse to me from the Bible?" someone asks. "Well, it was like all of a sudden a pounding began inside my heart. It was like God was knocking at its door—the very door of my soul!"

The more I try to do God's job, the more I get into endless arguments. I gave that up some time ago. Now the more I allow him to do his work while I concentrate on doing what I'm responsible for, the more effective my witness is.

Not everyone believed Jesus when he spoke those famous words of Matthew 5. But many did believe him when he said he was the light of the world—and that his committed followers were light, too. Thank God for them and for their faith, because in the midst of a vile period of human history, they went out and figuratively turned the world upside down.

Can the same be said of us?

As the beauty of Christ begins to transform the tough setting of our daily work, we can come to the place where we, too, can enjoy introducing him to others.

May we be worthy of the challenge he has given us!

D.M.

End-of-the-Day Replay

1. Remove distractions

2. Rerun the events of your day

3. Respond to Christ's evaluation

I sensed Christ said to me:

"This was well done: _____

_____

_____."

"Work harder on this: _____

_____

_____."

☐ To bridge the church/work gap I have completed one of the weekly assignments and recorded this information on page 216.

Introductions Take Work

Monday, Day Forty-Four

Christ wants to transform my daily work. Through today's Scripture, 2 Timothy 1:8-12, he is saying to me specifically,

"_____, *in your work situation*

_____

_____."

One of my responsibilities as high school student council president was to introduce guests at school assemblies. It was great training to say things like, "We are privileged to have as our Lyceum program speaker today a man with an amazing memory" or "This afternoon's assembly guest recently gave his scientific presentation at the world's fair."

Usually it wasn't hard to know what to say. I was given a printed sheet with a simple introduction provided by the guest. But one Friday our high school principal, Mr. Brockman, told me to expect a special guest the following Tuesday. Then he said the man's name in a way I was to know this guest was indeed important and that Mr. Brockman had done something special to get him to come. A United States senator—the honorable Paul Douglas!

On Monday, Mr. Daughty, my civics teacher, said, "David, I hear you get to introduce Senator Paul Douglas tomorrow."

"Yeah, I guess I do," I responded.

"What do you mean, you 'guess' you do?"

"Well, I think I do."

"What do you mean you 'think' you do, David? Aren't you ready yet?"

"I really hadn't thought about it," I confessed.

"Haven't thought about it? Do you know who Senator Paul Douglas *is*?"

"Y-yes," I stammered.

"All right, then! Get busy on what you're going to say. He's not an entertainer. We don't want a senior United States senator from Illinois, with a distinguished military record, visiting Quincy High School and not be introduced properly."

Something about Mr. Daughty's voice told me this Senator Paul Douglas was in a bigger league than the ornithologist who had come the month before, or the magician I'd get to introduce before the year was over.

That night I went to the library and checked out a book about the good senator. I read it and wrote out a three-paragraph introduction—sheer dynamite. Finally the big day came, went, and all went well. As I look back at that experience, three things jump out.

One: The senator told me after the assembly that my introduction was one of the best he'd been given for some time. (I should have given him my notes. He could have sent them to other high school student body presidents.)

Two: Mr. Daughty, my civics teacher, thought I was marvelous. I could have flunked his final and still gotten an A.

Three: I learned that making a good, original introduction can take a lot of work. But it's worth it.

Some people are good at introducing their friends and others aren't. Those who do it well were probably taught it or saw it modeled. It's a great skill, however it was learned.

On the negative side, have you ever been talking with someone when a third party comes up, known to your friend but unknown to you, and you're never introduced? You just stand there. And stand there. Makes you feel awkward, doesn't it?

Or has anyone ever introduced you but failed to give you any kind of identity other than your name? "Oh, by the way, Jim, this is

David." And then they go right on talking to each other. That's a little better, but it's still awkward.

What I want to bring up, of course, is how we introduce Christ to others. My guess is most believers agree they should be better at this than they are. But to make a good introduction of Jesus, especially at work, is going to take extra thought.

We have a wonderful friend to introduce. It's an honor. It's not an obligation or something to be frightened of or a task to make you look silly.

It's like when I finally realized, "Of all the students in this high school, I'm the one who was chosen to introduce Senator Douglas." Or like you saying, "Wow! I have going to work with me the most important personality this world has ever known. And he's my personal friend! I'd really like to introduce him to others the way he deserves to be introduced."

The only catch is, people can't see him. Or hear him. Or shake his hand. You'll have to figure out how to introduce Christ in a more subtle fashion than, "D-d-do y-you kn-know Jesus? He's my bestfriendwhosavedmeeversincethedayhebecame mypersonalsaviorbythegraceofGodexcept—uh—he's invisible."

I suggest you begin by introducing Christ through things people can see. Maybe you could say, "I read an interesting book the other day. Do you remember Charles Colson, the man involved in the Watergate scandal? He wrote this book and describes what's happened in his life since then. I'd like to discuss it with someone—would you be interested in reading my copy if I loaned it to you?" Or, "I read a magazine article about the religious faith of some of the presidential candidates. I have some thoughts about this topic. What do you think about it?"

These are ways to open a conversation which later might lead to introducing Christ without being too frontal. I do that a lot of times by saying, "Yeah, I'm a minister, but if you want to talk about spiritual things, the first conversation is always limited to two questions." Thinking about ways to introduce Christ is like me going to the library back in high school and thinking, *I need to take this assignment seriously.* It's worth the time to think about ways to make an effective introduction of our Lord.

Some ideas will work great and you can use them time and again. It may be as simple as, "Tell me what you did this last weekend." Usually the person will ask you the same question. Then you say, "Well, I go to church every Sunday morning, and that's good. I really like that you can have free coffee and a donut if you get there early enough. That way, when I go into the service I'm wide awake. And this Sunday I really sensed the Lord there."

The bottom line is, you try to figure out how you can get people to meet Jesus. And meeting Jesus is a lot more important than meeting a U.S. senator. For one thing, Jesus never leaves office.

D.M.

End-of-the-Day Replay

1. Remove distractions

2. Rerun the events of your day

3. Respond to Christ's evaluation

I sensed Christ said to me:

"This was well done: _____

_____

_____."

"Work harder on this: _____

_____

_____."

☐ I am remembering this week to give away three of the presents of Christ and to record this information on page 216.

Coming to Heaven Late

Tuesday, Day Forty-Five

Christ wants to transform my daily work. Through today's Scripture, Hebrews 12:2-14, he is saying to me specifically,

" _____, *in your work situation*

_____

_____."

A wine producer in need of additional help hired some migrant workers to gather his harvest. Early in the morning he found a number of extra hands and agreed with them on terms of payment.

Several hours later, seeing he didn't have enough manpower to get the job finished, he arranged for additional crew members. At noon, and again at three o'clock, he did the same thing. By five it was obvious the job was still too big, so hurrying into town to look for more help, he spotted some folks standing around. "How come you're not working?" he hollered. "No one's hired us," they yelled back. "Hop in and I'll keep you busy until sundown," he told them.

His final recruits were able to get in a little more than an hour's work. But when it came time to pay, the man gave everyone an entire day's wage, regardless of the hour the worker began. This delighted the ones who arrived late, but those who sweat through the entire day were indignant. "It's not fair!" they fumed.

"Wait a minute, now," came the reply. "I paid you exactly what we agreed upon. Take your money and go. Who are you to tell a man he can't be generous? I can do exactly what I want to with my money."

If you were one of the late starters, would you be pleased? Don't try to judge whether the employer was fair. Don't identify with the workers who started picking grapes early in the morning. Pretend you're one of those who didn't agree to work until late in the afternoon. How would you feel about your wages?

I confess I didn't read about this incident in a newspaper or magazine. The account appears in the Bible. It's one of the short stories told by Christ to make a point. If you're not familiar with it, you can look it up in Matthew 20.

The passage has nothing to do with fair employment practices. It's a story our Lord used to illustrate the rule of heaven. It teaches that certain people who get into heaven will have come to Christ early in life and will serve him long and hard. But others will receive the same privilege of heavenly citizenship even if they respond to Christ late in life and put in little service time. Does that seem unfair? I don't think so. No true Christian would say to the Lord, "Because that guy over there hasn't done as much for you as I have, I don't think he deserves heaven." I wouldn't say that and neither would you.

That's why I don't think it's important to identify with the workers who complained. I'm concerned there might be people reading this book who realize they might not be Christians. As they've looked into spiritual matters, suddenly it hits them. BAM! "What am I supposed to do now?" they ask. "My wife is on a spiritual adventure, but I'm not." Or, "The more I get into this adventure, the more I see that there's more than a gap between church and work. For me there's a gap between myself and the Lord." Or, "Here I am, getting on in years and on a fifty-day spiritual adventure about Christ transforming my daily work, and I'm not even sure if Christ has transformed *me*."

Hear me, friend. I've set aside today to address your need. We've been thinking about reaching out to others with the message of Christ, but what you need is someone to reach out to you.

"But I've lived this long," you say. "Maybe I still belong to the enemy. If there is such a place as the kingdom of heaven, I doubt I merit living there."

Many people in your situation reason that way. But then, what about this story Jesus told? What if his point was that heaven can be yours today as much as if you had responded to his call a long time ago? That would be great news, wouldn't it? In fact, of all the things you could be told today, what could possibly be better?

For so long you've put off settling this matter. And yet he still says, "Come!" and promises heaven. Why not take time today to make peace with him?

"I'm not sure I'd know what to say if I did," you respond.

Let me see if I can get you started. Appeal to the quality in God highlighted in this story. Why did the latecomers get paid what they did? Did they deserve it? No. It's that the vinekeeper was generous. Kind. Gracious. Merciful.

Instead of giving us what we deserve, God surprises us by handing us what we don't deserve. When you're guilty and the judge excuses you anyway, he's being merciful. Mercy—that's kindness in excess of what's expected.

So what do you say? You say, "God, I hear you're known for your mercy. And that's what I need. Lord, please be merciful to me, a sinner." Incidentally, you're not alone in this regard. The reason I've been forgiven by Christ and accepted into his kingdom is not because I deserve it. It's because God has been extremely kind to me. That's all.

The apostle Paul writes in Ephesians 2 that you're not saved by your own doing, it's a gift of God. Not because of hard work, lest anyone should boast.

Those who have waited long before coming to Christ should appeal to his mercy. Applied to you, that means your prayer should go something like this:

> God, I'm not used to asking someone to be merciful to me, kind, forgiving. But that's what I need right now. Forgive me, please, for my long delay, for my many sins. What I want is to be part of your kingdom. Enter my life, please, by your Holy Spirit, and make me fit for that. Thank you, Jesus.

Salvation is not a matter of the proper pay for the proper amount of work. Rather, it's that the one in charge shows us his mercy. Here's how the hymn writer captured it:

There's a wideness in God's mercy
Like the wideness of the sea;
There's a kindness in his justice
Which is more than liberty.

For the love of God is broader
Than the measure of man's mind,
And the heart of the Eternal
Is most wonderfully kind.

That says it well, doesn't it? Friend, begin with God's kindness and mercy when you talk with the Lord today. Either he is this way or he isn't. And the testimony of believers down through the centuries is that he most certainly is!

D.M.

End-of-the-Day Replay

1. Remove distractions

2. Rerun the events of your day

3. Respond to Christ's evaluation

I sensed Christ said to me:

"This was well done: _____

_____

_____."

"Work harder on this: _____

_____

_____."

☐ I remembered to pray the Ultimate Authority Prayer today.

228

Peak Performance

Wednesday, Day Forty-Six

Christ wants to transform my daily work. Through today's Scripture, Colossians 4:5-6, he is saying to me specifically,
"_____, *in your work situation*

_____ . "

What motivates you to give your best performance on the job? Money? The possibility of promotion? Maybe it's fear—you're afraid that if you don't perform well, you'll be let go.

I was an impressionable junior higher when my older brother left for college. He worried a lot about flunking out. That always confused me because he usually got straight *As*. Later I learned his motivation to get good grades was fear of bringing shame to the family name. He never has! In fact, now he has his doctorate.

Could it be that your motivation to excel on the job is love for your family? You want to be a good provider so you take care to fulfill your responsibilities as a spouse and parent.

Possibly it's your personality that drives you to excellence in your daily work. You take pride in what you do. By nature you're a perfectionist and it just goes against your grain to give anything but 100 percent.

In Matthew 25, Jesus tells us about two men who were highly motivated to excel in their work and one man who wasn't. An employer was about to take a long trip. Before he left he called together the three men who worked for him and gave them money to invest while he was away. He divided the money in proportion to their abilities.

To one man he gave five thousand dollars, to another two thousand, and to the last, one thousand dollars. The first two guys performed on the job because they wanted to please the boss. They worked hard, made some wise investments, and had doubled the money entrusted to them by the time their employer returned home.

Their boss reacted with praises and raises. "You've been terrific workers! I'm so pleased! You've been faithful in handling these small amounts, so I'm going to give you more."

But the third man was motivated by fear. He was afraid of his boss, known as a hard taskmaster with high expectations. The man's fear immobilized him. So he took the money entrusted to him and buried it, making sure he wouldn't lose it.

When his boss found out, he was furious. "At least you could have put my money in a bank and earned some interest!" And right on the spot the boss fired this irresponsible employee.

The two men motivated to please the boss were productive and excelled on the job. But the man who feared and disobeyed his boss was unproductive and got fired. He lost out completely.

The underlying point of this story is that believers are to recognize it's God who has given us certain skills and abilities. Bottom line, it's our job to use what we've been given in a way that pleases him.

The highest motivation we have to do the best we can in our daily work is to please our most important boss, the Lord himself. This is verified in Colossians 3:23-24: "Whatever you do, work at it with all your heart, as working for the Lord, not for men. . . . It is the Lord Christ you are serving."

There it is. I don't care who you are, the most important boss you have to please is Jesus. And when your priority concern is to please Jesus above all others, I can almost guarantee your other bosses will be satisfied as well. Your on-the-job performance is likely to peak when you affirm Christ as your most important superior.

When you follow through on the teachings of Christ by loving your neighbor, encouraging the timid, and looking out for the interests of others, it makes you a better worker. When you obey the commands of the Lord, speak truth, maintain integrity, and refuse to compromise standards of excellence, over the long haul you will win respect in the workplace.

The other day I received a new publication called *Marketplace Networks*. On the first page there was a section called "Standing Up to Office Politics." It included an article titled, "How Daniel Kept the Faith Even When the Boss Played Rough." It's a great article, and it reinforces exactly the point I'm making.

> While Daniel was surrounded by secular colleagues who were hostile to his faith and they tended to resent it when his values cramped their style, somehow Daniel's boss, the king, discerned that Daniel's bottom line was serving God. He came to understand Daniel's agenda and admired him for it.

There it is again, just like in Colossians 3. Daniel's bottom line was to serve the Lord above all others and eventually it paid off. His performance on the job peaked, and he became second in command over an entire nation.

In this same issue of *Marketplace Networks*, Christian businessman Kent Pucket says, "Stick to your guns, and someday you'll find yourself more secure in your career than your colleagues who allow themselves the luxury of taking the easy road to the top."

How do you stick to your guns? How do you affirm Christ as your most important superior? I'll tell you: by continuing to do what you've been doing for the past forty-six days in this spiritual adventure. Keep praying the Ultimate Authority Prayer. If it helps you, rewrite it. Make it more personal, put it in your words. But keep praying it. Let it be kind of a daily pledge of allegiance to your true superior.

Another way to affirm Christ as your most important superior: Continue to give away his presents. Believe me, when you give away presents like patience, kindness, joy, and self-control, over a period of time people are going to notice. You're going to make a positive difference in your place of daily work.

One final thought. In Proverbs 3, the Lord tells us, "Don't forget my teaching. Keep my commands in your heart." In other words, "Please me above all others. And as you do, you will win favor and a good name in the sight of God and man."

How's that for a motivating promise to help us excel in our daily work?

S.B.

End-of-the-Day Replay

1. Remove distractions

2. Rerun the events of your day

3. Respond to Christ's evaluation

I sensed Christ said to me:

"This was well done: _____

_____

_____."

"Work harder on this: _____

_____

_____."

☐ I have given away at least one of the presents of Christ this week and have recorded this information on page 216.

It's Not Working

Thursday, Day Forty-Seven

Christ wants to transform my daily work. Through today's Scripture, 1 John 2:6-11, he is saying to me specifically,

"_____, *in your work situation*

_____

_____. "

═══════

"Hey," you say, "it's day forty-seven of this spiritual adventure, and my job is still boring! I mean, it's unchallenging, meaningless, downright demeaning. Even to think about what I go through each week to get a paycheck makes me angry. So when's the great daily work transformation going to take place? We're running out of days!"

Today I'll try to answer that question.

To begin with, although I don't know what most of you do for a living, the one I represent does. He's aware of what shift you work, how much you make, when you began, the name of your boss (if you have one), the location of your office, the make of the semi you drive, what grade level you teach, your commission on sales last week, how the farm's doing, the union to which you belong—you name it, he knows it.

On top of that, his recall is better than yours. He understands the difficult personalities with whom you work better than you do, and he could express your internal struggles as accurately as you yourself can.

Being God doesn't remove him from relating to you on small matters like this. At this very moment, God knows not only the kind of employee or worker you are, he also knows if your job is below your capabilities.

"Wait a minute!" you say. "Where does the Bible say that God notices how we do our jobs?"

Colossians chapter 3, verse 22 says we should not only work hard when we're being watched, as "men pleasers," but we should do it as "fearing the Lord." Knowing that he too is observing all our actions, we should "work heartily." And Paul is writing here to people working in less than desirable conditions.

When a Christian is stuck in a job that doesn't satisfy, the unfulfilled party is told to work as though serving the Lord, not men. In other words, such people are to picture their work as something done on behalf of Christ.

"Big deal," you say. "What's that supposed to accomplish? It still ends up with me doing the same, stupid old thing!"

Maybe. I can't change your job for you, but I can promise you on the authority of Scripture that God will reward those who work as though they were faithfully serving him. Listen to the Bible itself: "Whatever your task, work heartily, as serving the Lord and not men, knowing that from the Lord you will receive the inheritance as your reward; you are serving the Lord Christ" (RSV).

"Oh, that all sounds so nice," you say, "supersweet, just the way preachers do it. 'Pretend you're working for Jesus, my dear friends, and POOF! Everything changes just like that!' Look, I don't know what kind of jobs people had back in Bible times, but I'll bet they were better than the underpaid, stupid thing I've ended up doing."

Not really. The class of people Paul was writing to were slaves. They did what they were told, regardless. They received nothing for it and their chance of change was far less than yours, even though they were as fully human as you.

Elsewhere, Paul says to slaves, "If you can legally gain your freedom, go ahead and take it. But until then, be God's person where you are by working as though serving him, even though your lot is unpleasant" (see 1 Corinthians 7:21).

That's what I'm repeating for you. If you can secure a better job, great! But until that time, because there's something inherently redemptive about good, honest work, fill your role as though you're doing it for Christ himself.

There is no such thing as a perfect job, anyway. No matter what you do, there will always be problems.

Some of you need to put to rest your quest for a vocation of pure bliss. It's nowhere to be found! You may think it sounds like the "Life of Riley" just to talk a few minutes several times a week on the radio as I do. But in ways unknown to those who have never done it, the role is both exhausting and sometimes frightening.

On the other hand, I might say that a person has it made who knows nothing about the pressures of deadlines and fund-raising and a staff to manage, but who leaves his troubles at some factory at 4:30. Some of you know otherwise . . . don't you?

I thank the Lord for my co-workers at the "Chapel of the Air" who have been consistently willing to do difficult and unheralded jobs with grace and style and dignity. Through the years, the Lord has graciously given me some of the finest people in the world. With the hundreds of thousands of mailings, phone calls taken one after another, donations recorded, errands run, last minute details covered, encouraging words offered, crises abated, situations soothed, sacrifices made, errors corrected, and on and on—the list staggers me! I thank God for these dear workers.

All the time they're pleasant beyond any reasonable expectation. Regularly they've gone far beyond what could have been asked. Had these people been working for Christ himself, I don't believe their performance would have been so different.

The truth is, I think that's what most of them *are* doing. They follow Paul's admonition to serve Christ even when the job is less than ideal. I just happen to be the human recipient.

A verse in Matthew underscores what I'm saying. It reads, "He who receives a prophet . . . shall receive a prophet's reward. And he who receives a righteous man . . . shall receive a righteous man's reward" (10:41, NKJV).

I take my hat off to all such folk. But their reward goes far beyond the thanks I can give them. God himself will properly compensate them.

Working for a radio minister is just one example of a tough job at less-than-average pay, but it illustrates that this is not as impractical as at first it may have sounded.

God *will* reward those who work as though they were faithfully serving him. "Whatever your task, work heartily, as serving the Lord and not men, knowing that from the Lord you will receive the inheritance as your reward; you are serving the Lord Christ."

It's a promise. And you can bet it will be kept.

D.M.

End-of-the-Day Replay

1. Remove distractions

2. Rerun the events of your day

3. Respond to Christ's evaluation

I sensed Christ said to me:

"This was well done: _____

_____

_____."

"Work harder on this: _____

_____

_____."

☐ I have established a support relationship with another Christian and am meeting at least once a week.

Miracle in the Making

Friday, Day Forty-Eight

Christ wants to transform my daily work. Through today's Scripture, Philippians 2:3-11, he is saying to me specifically,

"_____, *in your work situation*

_____

_____."

═══

I have to believe Jesus enjoyed his daily work. I presume it's satisfying to make something out of wood—a table, a cabinet, a wagon. Oh sure, working in the limited surroundings of a carpenter's shop might have been frustrating after having fashioned the plants and animals of our world and being responsible for the design and operation of our universe. But I still think Jesus liked his first job.

His second job—that of being the rightful king who would save the world—apparently generated some reservations.

It's hard for us to imagine the insane pounding of the soldiers who nailed our Lord's flesh to the rough-cut wood of the cross. No carpenter's finesse here, no careful balancing of function with beauty. Just a job someone was assigned to do in order to fulfill the wishes of the powerful.

I wouldn't have wanted his assignment: "He humbled himself and became obedient to death—even death on a cross!"

Yet the challenge in this passage from Philippians 2 is that we think like Christ, that his mind would be our mind—even when it comes to our daily work. We sing in church, "May the mind of Christ my Savior live in me from day to day," which I assume means Monday through Saturday as well as Sunday.

When we start thinking like Christ does, even about daily work we don't much like, we set ourselves up to experience something very good. Maybe a miracle in the making.

Our Lord established the pattern for us. Although his job was awful in certain respects, yet he submitted his thinking to his father in heaven. Because he did, in less than three days he was alive again from the dead, victorious—exalted by God to the highest place and given the name that's above every name "that at the name of Jesus every knee should bow, in heaven and on earth and under the earth, and every tongue confess that Jesus Christ is Lord, to the glory of God the father" (Philippians 2:10-11).

Talk about a promotion, an incredible turnaround! That's a fantastic success story, a vindication of having done what was right, a miracle of miracles. And it's *that* mind-set that we are to tap into. There's always a miracle in the making when you think Christ's thoughts about your daily work.

Awhile ago a faithful friend of the "Chapel" stopped by my office. He told me he felt my thoughts about this ministry were not always consistent with those of Christ. He believed the Lord wanted to bless the "Chapel," to use it in a manner far beyond my plans. He sensed that my goals were more restrictive, more cautious, more lacking in faith than they should be.

He wasn't asking me to think of ways to expand our outreach. He wanted me to try harder to discern the mind of Christ regarding the "Chapel of the Air," and then to submit to it.

I have to admit that regularly asking myself what Christ thinks about my daily work truly challenges my perspective. If anything, I've stopped working *for* Christ and begun more working *with* him.

I'm telling you this because a double miracle soon began to unfold. First, I became excited as I began to believe that Christ was not only pleased with the direction we had been headed, but that he wanted to bless us because he saw this work as strategic. I began praying new things, such as, "From now on, Lord, don't give us enough to get by. Bless the 'Chapel' abundantly. I believe you want to so we can do everything you have in mind for us."

That was a great shift for me.

Second, God has begun to do precisely this! It's been almost simultaneous with the shift in my thinking. In fact, my new problems as director of the "Chapel of the Air" include trying to figure out what to do because we're so cramped for space. We're bursting at the seams because of all God is doing.

Soon, I'm going to have to get in touch with some of Jesus' present carpenters to add to the back of our office; otherwise we're going to have to figure out how to put in bunk desks.

If I've been in ministry as long as I have and this challenge from my friend was something new to me, I have a feeling it's new for most of you, as well. To look at your job and say, "Jesus, what are your thoughts about my daily work? Let me tap into your thinking. I want to serve you, but more than that I want to know your mind regarding my work."

Maybe you're a homemaker who is dreadfully tired of laundry and fixing meals and housecleaning. Yes, you can do those faithfully as serving Christ—but I suggest you also start asking, "Jesus, what are your thoughts about my daily work? If I could think like you do about it, how would that change my outlook?" If you can do that and start living it out, you might even see the unfolding of something beautiful and miracle-like.

Salesperson, don't just pray, "Lord, help me to be faithful to you as I work," but, "Christ, what are your thoughts about my workday? Help me to have your mind." Pray such a prayer habitually, expecting that as the Lord exalted his Son, so will he those who think his Son's thoughts. Don't think of this as an extra job but as one of the fastest ways to see a miracle.

Are some of you like I was? You're serving Christ well, but not necessarily thinking his thoughts about your work as a coach, or a nurse, or a chef, or a navy pilot, autoworker, newspaper reporter. Christian, yes, but thinking too much like a normal human and not enough like the Son of Man.

As Christ had to experience the very worst of what he was called to do in his work, I believe the Father was saying, "Remember, Son, there's a great miracle ahead. It's not that far off. Can you hold to that belief?"

Now he's saying to some children of his Son, marked by Christ's Spirit alive in you, "Can you believe that, also? It's getting very near resurrection time."

If we can, I know that we can expect to see the unexpected. Maybe even a great move of Christ's Spirit through the churches of North America. I believe that's consistent with Christ's thoughts.

How wonderful that he's letting us be a part of what he's about. An incredible turnabout, another of his great success stories . . . a miracle of miracles.

D.M.

End-of-the-Day Replay

1. Remove distractions

2. Rerun the events of your day

3. Respond to Christ's evaluation

I sensed Christ said to me:

"This was well done: _____

_____

_____."

"Work harder on this: _____

_____

_____."

☐ This week I gave away three presents of Christ and recorded this information on page 216.

The Worker's Only Hope

Saturday, Day Forty-Nine

Christ wants to transform my daily work. Through today's Scripture, Leviticus 26:33-35, he is saying to me specifically,

"_____, in your work situation

_____

_____."

Three books about China have recently stirred me to consider how dangerous life is for the worker.

Life and Death in Shanghai is about a Chinese woman who suffered through the Cultural Revolution. Her home was destroyed, her daughter was murdered, and she was imprisoned. Somehow she survived to get out of China and write about it.

The Gate of Heavenly Peace is about the Chinese from 1895-1980. It looks at the revolution through the eyes of Chinese writers, many of whom were murdered. They would find themselves on one side of a faction or the other, the power scene would shift, and they would be murdered or beheaded or slaughtered or buried alive. It's a gruesome history.

Last I picked up *The Soong Dynasty*, about the most powerful and wealthy family in China. It details the power struggles in China in which millions were slaughtered. No matter which side came in to take over a territory, they would slaughter opposition groups.

Then when that group lost power, the next group would repeat the story.

Usually the revolutionaries came to power with the worker in mind: "We will bring in the best days for the working people." But this grab for power, in its very heart, depraves those who finally achieve. Always it's the working people who pay a horrible price. That's very clear through history, particularly the history of the last century. Not only have millions been slaughtered in China, millions have been butchered all over the world, from the Nazis to the fascists to the modern Marxist regimes. The more you read, the more despairing you become.

One part of *The Soong Dynasty* tells what happened in April, 1927. It tells about Chiang Kai-shek's forces, but it could have been written about any group that grabs for power.

One hundred thousand electric workers had walked off the job. Their unarmed protest planned to march to Chiang Kai-shek's headquarters. When they were some distance away, soldiers on both sides of the route opened fire with heavy machine guns. As the marchers tried to escape, Chiang's soldiers charged with fixed bayonets. Many people were pursued into private homes, dragged out, and bayoneted in the streets. The corpses filled eight trucks.

This reign of terror lasted for a week. Another eight thousand or so were killed the next week. Six thousand women and adolescent girls—wives and daughters of workers—were sold into the brothels and factories of Shanghai.

You read one thing after another and you just wonder. You hear the blood crying from the ground, your heart is heavy, and you lean toward despair. The inhumanity of man toward man is endless and unimaginable.

There is light in the darkness, however. These books don't even mention another revolution occurring at the same time. They don't talk about the growth of the church in China.

When the communists took over and Mao Tse-tung marched down from the north, Chiang Kai-shek fled with his nationalist troops. The country was closed and missionaries escaped or were expelled or murdered. All news of the church, estimated to be about 600,000 strong at the time, was cut off.

That was forty years ago. Recently we have discovered that during that time, in the most inhospitable environment and during

242

dreadful times, the church grew from 600,000 to at least six million—and some say closer to twenty million.[1]

Stories like this make it clear that the only revolutionary movement in the world that works is the one that begins in the human heart with redemption. And the only leader who can make it work is Jesus Christ, our Lord.

A great scripture about Christ and working people shows the total contrast that he brings to our world: "Come to me, all you who are weary and burdened, and I will give you rest. Take my yoke upon you and learn from me, for I am gentle and humble in heart, and you will find rest for your souls. For my yoke is easy and my burden is light" (Matthew 11:28-30).

Mankind, even with the best of intentions, is powerless to bring about revolutionary movements that will raise the status of humankind. It can only occur through Jesus Christ.

The future hangs in the balance. Is there hope or isn't there? If Jesus remained in the grave, these atrocities will be repeated again and again, endlessly. But if Christ really did rise from the dead, then there is hope, hope for the working man. The *only* hope for the working man.

A death impulse haunts the genetic system of mankind. When nothing prevents people from a total exercise of absolute power, they become demonic. There's a death impulse in these revolutionary movements.

It makes you look into your own heart and say, "What is the death impulse there?" I know that apart from the living Christ in my soul and heart, doing his work of redemption in me, there was enough nihilism, enough denial of beauty of life, enough self-centeredness, enough ability to focus selectively on the negative, that this death impulse would corrupt and eventually overcome me.

But I'm not that way any longer. Jesus has done something special—he conquered death and rose from the grave. I think of the hymn, "Lives again our glorious king, hallelujah! Where, O death, is now thy sting? Hallelujah! Dying once he all doth save. Hallelujah! Where thy victory, O grave? Hallelujah!"

The only hope for the world is Jesus. Christ is the worker's only hope, and as we are his representatives, we must be his change agents in the world. We must be convinced that we are the salt, even as he said.

To you who have examined the world and reached a point of despair, I say, "Christ in you is the hope of glory." As you take him into your workplace, as you allow him to integrate and infiltrate your daily life, that is a revolution of top order.

That Christ is unique and that he calls us into his service and into his family gives us hope. He is the true superior, and the worker's only hope.

Hallelujah!

D.M., K.M.

End-of-the-Day Replay

1. Remove distractions

2. Rerun the events of your day

3. Respond to Christ's evaluation

I sensed Christ said to me:

"This was well done: _____

_____

_____."

"Work harder on this: _____

_____

_____."

☐ I remembered to pray the Ultimate Authority Prayer today.

The Ultimate Sovereign
Sunday, Day Fifty

Christ wants to transform my daily work. Through today's Scripture, Colossians 1:15-23, he is saying to me specifically,

"_____, *in your work situation*

_____

_____ ."

It's not too smart to think less of a superior than you should. For example:

- You shouldn't have said your foreman was none too bright. Whether he was or wasn't doesn't matter. His hearing was good and he was standing close enough for your words to come through loud and clear.

- You made it known that, in your opinion, your coach didn't know very much about sports. But he was informed enough to know how to bench you until your thinking changed.

- As an executive, you acted as if the board of directors couldn't possibly get along without you. But they seemed anxious to prove they could.

- You agreed as a congregation that Jesus was adequate to fill certain roles, but before too long you felt his limitations began to show. So you needed to somehow compensate for his shortcomings.

Before we go any further, you need to know that this last scenario isn't merely hypothetical. It actually happened . . . in a New Testament church!

The church at Colosse is the group in question. The people there never actually forsook Christ; they only tried to add to what he could provide. They agreed he was a fine "sin-forgiver," but felt they needed something additional, something extra. They wanted secrets concerning the "deeper" matters of life. "Yes, Jesus performed his function well at the cross," they said, "but that was so limited. We need something more."

The apostle Paul got wind of this and wrote a strong letter to set things straight. He carefully laid out eight distinct points regarding this one who has been helping us transform our daily work:

1. Though no man or woman has ever seen God, we see his true likeness in Christ, the image of the invisible God (Colossians 1:15).

2. Christ shares the Father's matchless wealth—he is the firstborn of all creation (v. 15).

3. Jesus is the one who created our world, both the visible and the invisible parts (v. 16).

4. Jesus holds the key to "why." The meaning of life can only be explained by the Creator—it exists for him (v. 16)!

5. Jesus was, before any of it came into existence and continues as its sovereign. The crown still rests on his brow (v. 17).

6. Christ sustains the whole operation (v. 17).

7. Jesus is the head of the church. He gives it direction (v. 18).

8. Jesus is the first to come forth from the grave in power and glory, never to die again (v. 18).

Paul takes all eight of these points and says, "so that in everything [Christ] might have the supremacy" (v. 18).

How far can this be pushed? Look at verse 19. "God was pleased to have *all his fullness* dwell in him." No human being can have any greater ambition than to meet God. In Jesus Christ dwelt all the fullness of God. And we can know him personally!

Verse 20 says, "and through him to reconcile to himself all things." To reconcile means to bring together warring parties. God is reconciling to himself "all things, whether things on earth or things in heaven, by making peace through his blood, shed on the cross." To a congregation prone to apologize for poor, inadequate Jesus, the apostle lit up the skies with a dazzling display of spiritual facts.

Now the passage shifts. In the context of describing the wonder of our Lord, Paul now shows us Christ at his weakest—but, paradoxically, at his most glorious best.

The one whose mind conceived of trees for beauty, shade, fruit, and wood, was cruelly bound to a cross. The hands that spangled the heavens with countless, dancing galaxies writhed in pain from spikes that pierced them through. Taunted by rebellious subjects, the heir of the universe hung naked and pierced and motionless from a Roman cross. "He was in the world," wrote John, "and the world was made by him, yet the world knew him not." O, the wonder of it!

> And when I think that God, His Son not sparing
> Sent Him to die, I scarce can take it in;
> That on the cross, my burden gladly bearing,
> He bled and died to take away my sin:
>
> > Then sings my soul, my Savior God to Thee;
> > How great Thou art, how great Thou art!
> > Then sings my soul, my Savior God to Thee;
> > How great Thou art, how great Thou art!

No, it's never smart to think less of a superior than you should. This is especially true when it is the supreme authority in all the universe. What is smart is found in verse 23, "Continue in your faith, established and firm, not moved from the hope held out in the gospel."

There can be dire consequences at work when you think less of a superior than you should. But the consequences can be even more dire when you think less than you should of Jesus, who is supreme over all. Unfortunately, Colosse wasn't the only church with a limited view of Christ.

Let us once more consider the wonder of the person of Christ. Stand back and see him in all his splendor, in his supremacy, and be filled with awe at the mention of his name. *Jesus!* Let his personality capture you afresh, his magic prove delightful once again, his words explode in your heart. And respond, this last day of this fifty-day spiritual adventure, that Christ is all you hoped he would be . . . and more!

D.M.

End-of-the-Day Replay

1. Remove distractions

2. Rerun the events of your day

3. Respond to Christ's evaluation

I sensed Christ said to me:

"This was well done: _____

_____

_____."

"Work harder on this: _____

_____

_____."

☐ I remembered to thank the Lord for what he accomplished in my life the past fifty days.

Week Seven Notes ─────────────────

1. Lecture by David Aikonan, (correspondent in the Washington Bureau of *Time* magazine, specializing in foreign policy and communist affairs), Wheaton College, 27 January 1987.